FOOTNOTES TO A THEOLOGY

The Karl Barth Colloquium of 1972

edited and with an Introduction by

MARTIN RUMSCHEIDT

SUPPLEMENTS

FOOTNOTES TO A THEOLOGY

The Karl Barth Colloquium of 1972

edited and with an Introduction by

H. MARTIN RUMSCHEIDT

1974

The Corporation for the Publication of Academic Studies in Religion in Canada - La Corporation pour la Publication des Etudes Académiques en Religion au Canada.

ISBN — 0-919812-00-7

FOREWORD

The essays which are brought together here were originally delivered during the first colloquium of the Karl Barth Society of North America. It met at Victoria University in Toronto on October 26 to 28, 1972, and was entitled: The Theology of Karl Barth. The addresses by Markus Barth and Arthur Cochrane were given during the Colloquium Dinner; the others were more 'formal' and followed by at times very animated discussion.

During that colloquium the Karl Barth Society of North America was inaugurated. Its aim, far from being a personality-cult of Karl Barth, is to encourage a critical and constructive theology through the exploration of his work. It is envisaged that the assistance given to the Karl Barth Stiftung in Europe in its purpose to collect and preserve all literature by and about Karl Barth, the publication of a complete edition of his works together with the establishment on this Continent of a similar collection will make available for theological research materials that will adequately meet the proposed aim. Both the academic and the pastoral areas of theology are meant to benefit from the endeavours of this Society.

It is quite apparent that the aims of the Barth Society and of the Corporation for the Publication of Academic Studies in Religion in Canada overlap at certain points. The latter was founded with the specified purpose of "publishing a journal and other materials to serve the needs of scholars working in both the French and English languages in Canada in all fields of the academic study of religion". The Corporation is, therefore, pleased, that the directors of the Karl Barth Society have asked us to publish this collection of addresses. This volume is a part of those "other materials" referred to above: it is, indeed, a supplementary volume to the journal SR: Studies in Religion/Sciences Religieuses, published by this Corporation.

As I am 'wearing a director's cap' both of the Karl Barth Society and of this Corporation I am doubly pleased in the publication of this volume. As director of the former I thank my fellow board members for their readiness to have these addresses published by the Corporation, as president of the latter I thank my fellow directors of its board for accepting them as a supplement volume to our journal. With appreciation and pleasure I add an expression of thanks to those Canadian universities, religion departments and theological schools and colleges,

members of which belong sometimes to both this Corporation and the Barth Society, for their donations to the
Corporation in support of its aims, for it was that assistance which has made thinking seriously about publi-
cations supplementing SR possible.

> Martin Rumscheidt
> President
> The Corporation for the Publication
> of Academic Studies in Religion in
> Canada.

Contents

H. MARTIN RUMSCHEIDT

Introduction

'Footnotes to a Theology' - what an ambiguous title for
a publication of addresses delivered to a society whose
aim is said to exclude the veneration of him whose name
it bears. The Karl Barth Society of North America really
does not want to 'footnote' the 'master's' theology.
A negative declaration of intent does not, however,
help to explain the title of this volume. The explanation must begin with the assertion that the title refers to the addresses collected here and not to the
Society. What it wants to do has already been stated:
encourage critical and constructive theology through
exploration of Barth's work. It is clear to its members
that he left a legacy to the Church and to the community
of scholars whose work is the study of theology and of
religion. That this legacy does not have to be taken
seriously simply because it is Karl Barth's is also
clear, just as much as that it cannot be ignored. But
there will be a parting of minds over why the exploration of his work is fruitful for critical and constructive theology today. There are those who believe that
the attention Barth's work demands is due to "the fact
that for him priority in the process of theological
understanding lay exclusively and all-pervadingly on
the Word of God in Christ, who makes his Word heard to
those who, through the Holy Spirit, are attentive to
the Scriptures."[1] This concentration on the Word as
object of theology is regarded here as a passion for
objectivity; Barth's unrelenting circling around the
Word manifests the pathos of an objective scientist.
Factors as these are held up as reasons why his work
not only calls for but indeed deserves serious attention.
To others Barth's attractiveness lies more in his
critical iconoclasm or in his insistence that all theological assertions are parabolic or analogical in nature
and are not immediately or directly representative of
the truth theological understanding seeks to grasp.
Such people can take Barth seriously without accepting
his assertion that the Word is the determinative object
of the theological endeavour or without agreeing to the
individual conclusions to which Barth came on his own
critical and constructive road. "Either we must enter

1

with him into a vision of the unlimited sovereignty of
God's grace that reduces all else to negativity, finding
this vision as the uniform message of the Bible, or we
are forced simply to confess that this vision is not
real for us and that we must stand outside the circle
of faith defined by it. Few men in our age or any age
have come so near in confronting us with a final choice
for or against faith. If Barth has failed, as I believe he has, his has been one of the most brilliant
failures of all times."[2] Yet such 'outsiders', as the
author of this quotation would consider himself, do see
the need to take Barth seriously. Thus, to speak of
'footnotes to a theology' is, indeed, not to describe
the outlook of the membership nor to define the aims of
the Karl Barth Society of North America. The Society
surely ought to include 'right' and 'left' wing Barth
interpreters.

The authors of these addresses do not conceal the
fact that the man Karl Barth attracted them and that
his work did have an impact on theirs. Whether a son
would say that his relationship to his father is defined by the latter's winsome personality and powers of
thought is left unexplored, precisely because Markus
Barth refrained more than the others from such auto-
biographical comments or even indirect hints. All warned
against 'footnoting'. There really can be no mere explaining of the theology of Karl Barth, because neither
such explaining nor that theology is an end in itself.
If the editor nevertheless chooses that title he wishes
to underscore the implicitly held view that illumining
Barth's work and influence is one way of moving with
him and beyond him in the interest of a critical and
constructive theology for our times.

It is not necessarily self-evident that a variety of
addresses as the seven in this volume do have a common
focus or intent other than that which the title of the
Colloquium itself suggested: the theology of Karl Barth.
But that is no focus at all, unless one is prepared to
speak similarly of the whole side of a barn as a target
for precision-shooting. Yet all the way from Minear's
Barth vs. the Exegetes to Lamirande's The Impact of
Barth on the Catholic Church, from McLelland's Family
Affair to Cochrane's The Barth I Knew there is this
conviction: the theology of Karl Barth is of interest
because of the sort of questions he raised. "What are

the prospects of Christianity today? What has it to say
today and tomorrow in face and in the midst of the cata-
clysmic changes in which humanity is engulfed? How is
Christianity to hold its own in competition with and under the assault of newly arisen political religions and
reinvigorated older religions? How is it to fulfil its
mission in the technical world of the future? What is
Christianity, the Gospel, Christian faith? In Barth's
writing there is no practicable prescription for answering these questions. He is not indeed the only one to
face them and to say important things regarding them."3
We, too, must face them, in fact, how could we fail to
do so anyway? The interest which the authors of the addresses show in Barth's work is evidently nourished more
by the resoluteness and sustaining power of the way he
faces those and other questions than exclusively by his
answers to them. And yet one cannot deny that that resoluteness and sustaining power do account for the fact
that many of Barth's answers are not only important in
the eyes of many but also right.

Paul Minear illuminates the rather curious lack of dialogue between Barth's 'commentary' on Romans and nearly
the entire guild of St. Paul's recent exegetes. Is there
too deep a hiatus between the technical, scientific exegesis of Scripture and the theological one? Is Harnack
right when he insists that the theological professorship
must not be confused with the pulpit ministry?[4] Of course,
Barth had dethroned the gods of the seminar-rooms, as
Minear puts it, the gods of Minear's own guild. That may
very well have been an iconoclastic stroke, but was it
constructive for the task at hand - the understanding of
a man of ancient times? Paul Minear states that it was,
because it shook the understanding of time, of temporality, and of history loose from the insufficient, two-
dimensional view held by these scholars and called attention to a sense of time in St. Paul's writing with which
not only Barth, but in his quite different way also
Bultmann, and more recently such literary figures as
G. Poulet and A. Mendilow were struggling. Minear does
not subscribe to Barth's own proposed solution to that
problem of time, but then that is not the point. At
issue here is rather the realization that Barth's bomb-
shell on the theologians' playground prevents those who
are playing there now from losing track of time, especially
their own.

INTRODUCTION

Any modern-day Tertullian might well ask: what does
Karl have to do with Heinrich? substituting personal for
geographical names. Joseph McLelland, who is certainly
no Tertullian, speaks of a family affair in trying to
answer that question. His essay shows that the two
brothers, who both held chairs at the same university,
owed much to each other in their understanding of and
approaches to the other's discipline. Apparently neither
removed the insignia of his guild before engaging the
other. What would that suggest about the much argued
problem: Karl Barth and philosophy? It remains an impossible dream to show that Karl Barth was, after all,
'really' open to philosophy. What becomes clear in
McLelland's address is the Barthian dilemma - to insist
on the ancillary position of philosophy in the exercise
of theology but yet to make cheerful use of philosophy
in its critical, epistemological task. But can one ask
that seriously of philosophy? This question, raised by
McLelland, is illumined by the family affair. He reveals the Kantian underground, the 'synthetic a priori'
in both men's views of their respective and each other's
disciplines. And that loads the definitions of philosophy
and theology unduly in one direction. Is the Kantian
understanding the only one? Of course not, but it is
the one Barth works with and which he places in opposition to theology as 'the most beautiful of all sciences'.
The dialogue of these opposites in Barth's work is ambiguous, yes self-deceiving, concludes McLelland. But
it does move theology, at times also Barth's, to what is
called limiting concepts where there arise better perspectives on the relation of philosophy and theology as
well as a <u>Mitmenschlichkeit</u> of their representatives in
terms of humour.
Thomas Mendip's declamation "O tedium, tedium, tedium...
Where in this small talking world can I find a longitude
with no platitude" leads to the centre of Paul Lehmann's
search for concreteness in theology. In his own words,
why is our theological existence today devoid of persuasive and freeing concreteness and vulnerable to idolatrous and cultic concreteness filling the vacuum in our
theological discrimination? Clearly there is today a
preoccupation with concreteness in theology and it is
just as earnest as was Barth's and Bonhoeffer's. Yet
exactly the preoccupation of these men brings the current
search for concreteness to a critical juncture, for they

4

are being asked now to show how to make sense of Jesus
Christ in the midst of a culture and experience of the
world come of age, whereas they ask theologians now to
make sense of the culture and experience of that world
come of age with due regard to the concrete pressure
and presence of Jesus Christ in our midst. Lehmann's
discerning discussion of the Barth-Bonhoeffer relationship sheds much light on the history of recent theology
and that alone is worthy of 'footnoting'. But his
motive and goal are something different; it is the urgency of a theological existence today at our concrete
place where we are called to be, or in different words,
it is the unavoidable necessity of the search for a
faith for being human in the similarly unavoidably
necessary struggle against the mounting arrogance and
brutality of power. Such a faith comes as a consequence
of concreteness in theology and would indeed be a longitude without platitudes.

Markus Barth's address is a report on a very vigorous
debate about what really matters in Karl Barth's theology.
The lines of the protagonists are clearly drawn so that
one may well speak, as in the case of Hegel's followers,
of right-wing and left-wing Barthians. To the one the
determinative object is the subject of Jesus Christ, the
revelation of God to man and it is the progressive penetration into the mystery of Jesus Christ, so obvious in
Barth's thought, which warrants that conviction. To the
others Barth's discovery of God's revolution and its
acme - the resurrection of the dead and the establishment
of God's kingdom on earth - precedes the discovery of
Christ's centrality. Christology, however necessary a
feature for Barth, does not replace what is essential
for him: God and the proletariat. A debate like that
cannot really be called a 'footnote to a theology'. On
the other hand the label does apply because in that debate there lurks much the question of the practical task
of Christian theology: what is the proclamation of Jesus
Christ, or what is discipleship?

Michael Wyschogrod had introduced the phrase: why is
the theology of Karl Barth of interest? For him it was
a matter of discerning why Barth is of interest to a
Jewish theologian. His answers were not meant to commend
Barth to all theologians. But Wyschogrod believes himself
to be in the presence of a member of the family simply because Barth is so scriptural, so humbled by the largely

5

Jewish Word of God, which Wyschogrod paraphrases as the
witness to a movement of God toward man. One reads in
his address that Barth, unlike Bultmann, is no gentile,
one in whose theology some alien frame of reference,
such as alleged verities of reason, can prescribe or
even anticipate God's decisions. If he is no gentile
then what is Barth? He is a Christian, says Wyschogrod,
someone who, even though a member of the family, differs
because his faith regarding the free and sovereign act
of the God of Israel is different from that of the Jewish
member of the family. Wyschogrod can best illuminate
that difference with the suggestion that in some respects
Judaism is more Barthian than Barth! What a footnote
that is! But Michael Wyschogrod tempers his appreciation
with some stinging criticism. He cites a lengthy enumer-
ation of the attributes Barth applies to the synagogue.
Here the spectre of anti-semitism arises and that, to
say the least, has become one of the thorniest problems
of theology and theological existence today. To be constructive in our time, the thought and existence of the
theologian must overcome a past in which it was not only
possible to ignore Jews but, indeed, to do away with them
on the ground of arguments theologically 'justified'.
    The next address, that of Emilien Lamirande, offers a
comprehensive picture of how those, whom Barth on the
whole regarded as the more alert critics of his work,
responded to it. But then it is often quite helpful to
discern the accents of someone's thought by looking at
the way the protagonists sich auseinandersetzen. (Cassell's
Dictionary renders that as 'coming to terms with'.) But
since it is a fact that as soon as someone has spoken a
word he can no longer claim sole possession of and jurisdiction over it but must now let it subject itself to the
understanding of his hearers, attention to such Ausein-
andersetzungen itself is part of the process of understanding, of critique and of being timely.
    The focus of only one of the addresses gathered in this
volume, Arthur Cochrane's, is Karl Barth the man rather
than his theology. Yet Cochrane wisely warns at the end
of his warm appreciation of the man Karl Barth that devotion to theologians must never take the place of concentration on the truth theology seeks to grasp. For
this warning, Cochrane cites Karl Barth himself as his
'authority' - it is a source of great amusement to the
angels when men try so hard to 'footnote' other theologians

instead of becoming wounded, like Jacob, in wrestling
with the God who is with men.

All of these essays, attempts to understand Karl Barth,
seek to further the much more daring attempt, namely man's
speech concerning God. That this attempt will go on,
critically, constructively and with real Mitmenschlichkeit,
namely with humour, is the wish of this volume and of the
Karl Barth Society.

NOTES

1 Heinrich Vogel, Freundschaft mit Karl Barth, Zürich,
   T.V.Z. Verlag, 1973, p. 68
2 John B. Cobb, Jr., Living Options in Protestant Theology, Philadelphia, Westminster Press, 1962, p. 197
3 Karl Barth, Church Dogmatics, ed. by Helmut Gollwitzer,
   New York, Harper and Row, 1962, p. 2f
4 Martin Rumscheidt, Revelation and Theology-An Analysis
   of the Barth-Harnack Correspondence of 1923, London,
   Cambridge University Press, 1972, p. 36

PAUL S. MINEAR

Barth's Commentary On The Romans, 1922-1972;
Or Karl Barth Vs. The Exegetes

During the past five decades the cleavage between the
biblical and the theological disciplines has steadily
widened, in accordance with the curricular demands of
highly departmentalized universities. Few historians
attempt the theological task; few dogmaticians attempt
the exegetical. Not so Barth. Seldom has a theologian
so fully immersed himself in the historical problems,
wrestling responsibly with the endless hermeneutical
challenges posed by the Scriptures. Each single volume
of the Dogmatics has more sustained exegesis, usually
in the fine print, than do most volumes produced by biblical historians. Yet biblical scholars have either
ignored or deplored this cultivation of their own domain.
Why? We may find an answer by exploring the early stages
of the encounter and then examining the situation near
the end of the half century.
    In spite of an abundance of first-hand sources, it is
difficult to recapture the barometric pressures prevalent
during the early stages of the conflict, between 1915 and
1925. Efforts to recover those pressures remind us of
how anachronistic historical work is bound to be. For
one thing, our interest in that early decade is a product
of later developments, and we cannot erase knowledge of
them from our minds in our effort to turn the clock back.
Even the phrase "the early Barth" guarantees a distortion
in the portrait by reflecting later history. The man
himself recognized this. As early as 1932 he wrote, "When
I look back at the book (Romans) it seems to have been
written by another man to meet a situation belonging to
a past epoch."1
    It was the change in his vocational situation which,
among other things, made Barth himself the first post-
Barthian. In 1932 he was a professor of theology. In
1918 he had been an individual Christian pastor, who had
suddenly uncovered a strange world in the Bible where God
had spoken to him with compelling authority. As most of
us know, there is a vast difference between reading the
Bible as a person crying out for divine help and studying
it as a professor. Few of us can measure that distance

8

because our own encounters with the Bible have for so
long been oriented toward meeting professional demands.
Yet there is a difference. Failure to recognize it is
one of the few defects in Brevard S. Childs' The Crisis
of Biblical Theology. Childs treats the various leaders
in the early biblical theology movement as if they wanted
"to form a school or devise a system"[2] whereas it was
actually the initiative of the Bible in answering their
cries for deliverance which forced them off the treadmill
of system-building. The power of this initiative is
neglected when the movement is characterized simply as a
shift in the mode of biblical studies.[3] Let us remember
that Barth's Commentary was primarily the work of a young
pastor, seeking to meet the needs of his parish.

We also should remember the familiar but frequently
ignored fact that history, though written backward, is
lived forward. Facing the unknown future at the point of
decision-making involves a different perception of the
temporal process than when a person looks back at known
decisions and known results. Looking back at Barth's
Commentary we activate a sense of time different from
that which was released in Barth as he read the Epistle
of Paul. The same fifty years means to the earlier
author something different than to the later historian.
Retrospect does change things. Some of us, in looking
back, are tempted to glorify that earlier situation,
building the tomb of this particular prophet, in spite
of the profound warning of Jesus against such tomb-
building (Mt.23:29f.). Others are tempted to exaggerate
the distance we have traveled since Barth, thus making a
desperate effort to keep up-to-date or even to reach the
future ahead of time. Many scholars have celebrated the
beginning of the post-Barthian epoch, beginning as early
as 1928 when a German journal announced that Barth "is
already slipping into the position of a man of yesterday". To this, Barth replied: "Dead men ride fast but
successful theologians ride faster". (Commentary, p.26)

This difference in time perspectives is even more
acute when the modern historian deals with the apostle
Paul. Imbedded in historical methodology is a sense of
time foreign to Paul. Of this collision Barth became
aware in his reading of the Epistle to the Romans. In
fact, it was his effort to do justice to Paul's consciousness of time that alienated professional exegetes. Where
Barth was willing to adapt his perception of time in order

9

to grasp Paul's message, his exegetical colleagues were
unwilling to do so.

The early stages in this development come clear in the
correspondence of Barth with Eduard Thurneysen, so use-
fully made available by James D. Smart: Revolutionary
Theology in the Making. Barth and Thurneysen had first
met as students, studying under Wilhelm Herrmann at
Marburg; then they had become pastors of churches in
neighboring Swiss villages, Safenwil and Leutwil. Soon
after they began their pastorates, the First World War
broke out, involving the universities in which they had
been studying. Their revered theological mentors joined
voluntarily in public declarations of support for the
Kaiser, a support which shocked the young pastors.[4] To
them it indicated a pollution of Protestantism by nationalism and secularism. As Barth wrote to his friend on
Oct. 15, 1915: "Everything that has to do with the state
is taken a hundred times more seriously than God."[5]
They recognized that the very word God, as used so glibly
by the churches, had lost its meaning; this God had died.[6]
And of his theological teachers, Barth wrote: "I suddenly
realized that I could not any longer follow either their
ethics and dogmatics, or their understanding of the Bible
and history."[7] The two pastors were forced by events to
see themselves standing outside Protestantism, unable
longer to belong to any group or school.[8] If the methods
of reading the Bible did not provide protection against
such perversions of the Gospel, something must be seriously wrong with those methods. (A similar observation
can be made regarding theological education in every
decade since). Here lies a major root of Barth's alienation from his exegetical colleagues.

Standing thus "outside Protestantism", the two pastors
focussed their attention on the Bible and on the needs of
their parishioners. "I tried to find my way", Barth wrote,
"between the problem of human life on the one hand and
the content of the Bible on the other."[9] Exegesis-as-
usual was replaced by "a cry for rescue", a cry which
could be compared to the cry of shipwrecked men, who had
lost everything and were floundering in the waves. When
their cry was answered, the "joy of discovery" separated
them even further from the academicians. The more vigorous their own conversations with the Bible, the more
sterile seemed the patterns of interpretation which they
had inherited. They had moved into a world which seemed

10

altogether different from the world of their exegetical
mentors. In a letter of Oct. 6, 1921, Thurneysen wrote:
"What kind of an earthquake region is this into which we
have stumbled quite unconsciously in the very moment
that we decided we had to read the New Testament a little
differently and more exactly than our teachers."[10]
The new situation might be symbolized in terms of the
number of desks at which they prepared their weekly sermons. Before they entered the "earthquake region" they
had used two desks: one where they examined the text as
the object of historical research, trying first of all
to reconstruct the ancient situation; the other where
they read the Bible spiritually and devotionally, listening for a message from God for his people.[11] But as successive Saturdays went by, these pastors found the separation of the two desks intolerable. Work at one desk
pushed the Bible farther and farther back, making its
world very strange and very old. Meanwhile at the other
desk volcanoes were erupting and thunders rolled. Because the very strange world insisted on invading the
present as a new and a true world, the two desks could
no longer remain separate. This was not simply a matter
of feeding suppressed desires; at times Barth would have
preferred the earlier arrangement: "I am in haste for
the time being to close the New Testament at this point
and to busy myself with passages in which the fire does
not burn so disturbingly."[12]
Thus the letters disclose the emergence of those attitudes toward the Scriptures which alienated Barth from
the exegetes. Further light on this emergence is provided by lectures delivered by Barth during the years
when the Commentary was gestating.[13] In these lectures
Barth made very clear his evaluation of contemporary
historical methods as applied to the Bible. On the one
hand, he affirmed his reliance upon "the established
results" of those methods. He agreed with that axiom of
historical study, first expressed by J.A. Ernesti in
1732, that the Bible must be studied like any other human
document. "It can lay no a priori dogmatic claim to
special attention."[14] On the other hand, he challenged
the adequacy of that principle in a strategic sentence,
which in effect cancels it. "Intelligent and fruitful
discussion of the Bible begins when the judgment as to
its historical and its psychological character has been
made..." Nothing could be more conventional than that;

it tips the hat to the prevailing deities of the academy.
But the sentence continues: "Fruitful discussion begins
...when the judgment as to its human...character has
been made and put behind us."[15] Those added words are
anything but conventional; they dethrone the gods of the
seminar room. The historian was bound to ask: "Why
should all such judgments be put behind us before fruitful discussion can begin?". To this protest Barth gives
a double reply. 1: The battle with "stark orthodoxy has
been put behind us". 2: This human document has a
"special content" which requires special treatment.[16]

This special content consists of the presence in the
Bible of God's world, the world of beginnings and endings,
"the deepest, innermost, surest fact of life."[17] In dealing with this world, critical reason is incompetent. "The
reason sees the small...but not the large. It sees the
preliminary, but not the final, the derived but not the
original, the complex but not the simple...what is human
but not what is divine."[18] The usual historical method
may be able to grasp the human problems and questions,
but it cannot lay hold of "the righteousness of God". It
is designed to explore a zone of reality where God is
absent and inactive, not the zone where God dwells with
men and acts to save them.[19]

As Barth pictured the situation, the exegete stands at
a window inside a house, watching the passersby in the
street. Suddenly those passersby stop, look up into the
sky, shade their eyes as they follow something hidden by
the roof from the watcher inside the house. What do
these men in the street see? "Something which is above
everything, which is absolutely beyond the range of my
observation and the measure of my thought."[20] Barth was
himself fascinated by this discovery, and his whole
Commentary reflects his fascination. "What a new world
it is...And how remote we still are, merely in the outer
court of this new world."[21] To Barth none of the biblical
authors was more aware of that world - closed to the controls of the historical method - than was Paul: "Paul --
what a man he must have been...The Reformers, even Luther,
are far from the stature of Paul...and then, behind Paul:
what realities those must have been that could set this
man in motion in such a way."[22] The "special content" of
this document forces the interpreter to face problems for
which the historical method has left him unprepared. With

what categories does he deal with the realities "behind
Paul"? When we consider the enigmatic character of
those realities, as well as the excitement of discover-
ing them, it does not seem strange that Barth should
rely upon negations: "Biblical religious history has the
distinction of being in its essence, in its innermost
structure, neither religion nor history -- not religion
but reality, not history but truth."[23] The reason for
reliance on paradox is perfectly clear: this history is
not history, this religion is not religion. It is wrong
to dub the realities either historical or unhistorical.
The categories do not fit the reality: "Biblical history...is not really history at all, but seen from above
is a series of free divine acts, and seen from below a
series of fruitless attempts to undertake something in
itself impossible."[24] Thus in his early lectures Barth
posed the problems which lay at the heart of his
Commentary and at the core of his debate with his exegetical colleagues. Incidentally it was these same
lectures which first introduced me to Barth's thought
and which forced me to recognize within the Bible a
"history which is different from all other histories,"
a history which therefore escapes the sieve of contemporary historians.[25] It is one thing, of course, to
recognize the presence of God in human events, and quite
another thing to know how to describe it. "When God
enters, history for the while ceases to be, and there is
nothing more to ask, for something wholly different and
new begins -- a history with its own distinct grounds,
possibilities and hypotheses...We may not deny nor prevent our being led by Bible 'history' far out beyond what
is elsewhere called history."[26] Barth is by no means
consistent in describing this reality: he may call it on
occasion the non-historical, the history that is not
really history, "true history", or simply history in in-
verted brackets.

   In analyzing such antitheses, we may observe that the
base-line of concepts is provided by the term history.
Because the meanings of this term are protean, the anti-
thetical terms will have multiple connotations. Until
one meaning is nailed down, its opposite will blow loose.
Barth accentuated the contrast without carefully nailing
down the foil of his thinking. We may assume that the
term "history" normally refers to that zone of reality
which is amenable to the operation and controls of the

13

historical method as applied by the professional historians of the day. Because so much escapes the net of
that method, "the word history implies limitation and
corruption." (Commentary, p.85). At any rate, the zone
of reality covered by that method remains very narrow
and thin. Not so the zone of reality to which the term
"biblical history" refers. This reality exerts an ultimate and absolute claim. As such, it has its own "distinct grounds, possibilities and hypotheses". The usual
modes of research are not capable of dealing with this
'history'. In fact, so long as scholars limit their
exegesis to the application of those modes, they distort
the reality to which the Bible witnesses. The result is
this: "The history of religion has become the history of
the untrue in religion, so that the truth becomes its
non-historicity." (Commentary, p.69·). As T.H.L. Parker
concludes: "The whole concept of history associated with
the historical method comes under assault."[27]

There is an informative contrast between Barth and
Bultmann in these early days; it becomes clear in com-
paring Barth's lectures with Bultmann's programmatic
essay "The New Testament and Mythology."[28] Both men
stressed the strangeness of the Bible; both were primarily concerned with the zone of eschatological truth.
Both mounted astute attacks on contemporary forms of
orthodoxy and liberalism. Both were keenly aware of the
limits of the historical method in dealing with the
message of the New Testament. However Bultmann conducted
no such assault upon conventional historical methodology,
but rather used it in such a thorough way as to command
the respect of his colleagues. He did nothing to
threaten the privileges or property rights of objective
scholarship. He found in Heideggerian existentialism a
way of dealing with the "wider" zone of reality that did
not require an attack upon the assumptions concerning the
historical process which were basic to the historian's
work. Bultmann has had legions of followers, exegetes
who have accepted his reconstructions of early church
history, quite apart from their endorsement of his "theology". But Barth has had very few partisans among the
exegetes, who have generally responded to his assault on
their views of history by building a solid wall of defence. They have felt that his theological assumptions
invalidated his historical work. They have refused to
accept him as an exegete, being delighted to uncover

numerous bizarre examples of eisegesis in his Commentary. The root of this impasse, I suggest, may be found in the contrary conceptions of history and of the temporal process which are imbedded in the dominant historical method.

Turning our attention now to the Commentary we will focus on one small segment, the treatment of Romans 13: 8-14. We select this text even though at first sight it seems to have no bearing on the problem of time and history. The text simply presents the demand for the love of neighbor as a way of fulfilling the Law. What is unusual about that? It is not surprising that most commentators deal with the text in an innocuous and banal fashion. Paul, however, relates this demand to a peculiar time-sense: "for now is our salvation nearer than when we first believed". To Paul, love is the measure of whether a person is living in the day or in the night. Even with this qualification, the command remains for most readers a pious convention. But Barth's seismograph detects beneath the surface of the text a volcanic disturbance. In the work of love, interrupting the normal flow of events, the two worlds, the two histories, are conjoined. Because it betrays an absolutely strategic relation between man and God, love is an "extremely enigmatic conception." (p.492). The love of neighbor becomes a test of our knowledge of God, the only mode in which we may love God. What is done to the neighbor, in all its mystery and untraceability, discloses what God has also done. In each work of love, therefore, there is a decisive theological coefficient.

There is an equally decisive Christological coefficient through the fact that the movement of Christian love is a response to the command of Christ. The victory of Christ was a victory of his love; the believer's obedience links him to that victory. It "points to the victory which has occurred, does occur, and will occur in Christ" (p.498). This makes the action of love an "essentially revolutionary action", in which the day of the Lord dawns, "the end of the world of time and things and men -- which is the Beginning" (p.498).

There is also a pneumatological coefficient in every deed of Christian love, inasmuch as it is a gift of the Spirit. Only the power of the Spirit can turn what is a religious impossibility into the possibility of God, i.e., the fulfilling of the Law (pp.493,494). Love is "the

existential standing-before-God of men, their being
touched by His freedom, whereby their personalities are
established" (p.493). So love becomes an event in that
history which transcends the Law, religion and everything
that is "capable of analysis and description" (p.494).

By discerning these trinitarian dimensions in the work
of love, Barth also discerned its eschatological ramifi-
cations. Since in love the old is overthrown by the
doing of the new, this action marks the very dissolution
of the course of the world (p.492f). Both the neighbor
and the lover are introduced into a strange new world.
Although this event is no moment in time, it becomes a
parable of the eternal moment (p.497). Love proclaims
"what hour it is"; by making visible the invisible new
age, it becomes an incomprehensible, miraculous event
between the times. In fact, something happens to time
itself. The lover realizes that "it is not time that
goes and comes; man it is who has been and will be in
God, who dies and lives" (p.497). The same lover will,
of course, recognize distinctions between near times and
far, for the action of love requires such distinctions.
But the tensions to which love attends are not those which
can be measured by years and centuries, but are those
which emerge from the contact between the temporal and
the eternal. Love is an awakening from sleep to see the
dawning of the Lord's day. This day is not "one period
of time succeeding another" but eternity itself (p.500).
Love has its own way of measuring the nearness of salvation. When Paul speaks of salvation as being nearer than
before (13:11), Barth argues that this "has as much or as
little to do with the well-known 1900 years of the history of the church...as it had with those weeks or months
during which the Epistle...lay in Phoebe's trunk" (p.499).
In such comments, Barth consciously challenged conclusions
which had been current coin among biblical scholars since
Wrede, Weiss and Schweitzer. More significantly, he repudiated the concept of linear time which has been assumed in modern historiography and which has been all
too naively read back into the New Testament authors.
There is hardly a scholar who does not attribute to Paul
the notion of an end of the world, to be located on an
objective time-line. Barth attacks them all: "The End of
which the New Testament speaks is no temporal event, no
legendary 'destruction' of the world; it has nothing to
do with any historical, or 'telluric', or cosmic catastrophe.

The End of which the New Testament speaks is really the
End; so utterly the End that in the measuring of nearness or distance our 1900 years are not merely of little,
but of no importance...Who shall persuade us to depress
into a temporal reality what can be spoken of only in a
parable?...What delays its coming is not the Parousia
but our awakening" (p.500). That awakening, Barth adds,
is a matter of daring to love God and neighbor, that
knowledge of the times which is expressed by readiness
to stand on the frontier between time and eternity (p.501).
   Parenthetically, let me remark on the character of
Barth's debt to Kierkegaard. Much has been made of
Barth's reliance, in his Commentary, on Kierkegaard's
"infinite qualitative distinction between time and eternity" (p.10). Later on, Barth realized the inadequacy of
that distinction, and, as we shall see, replaced it with
the category of eternal time. I find even more significant, however, Barth's agreement with Kierkegaard in using
the works of love as the best clue to the character of
New Testament eschatology. In this respect Barth did not
change. A study of the nexus between love and time in
the two authors would prove worthwhile.[29]
   Barth's treatment of love in Romans 13 shows how far
his objectives differed from those of other exegetes.
For him nothing displaced the desire for knowledge of God.
"Paul knows of God what most of us do not know; and his
Epistles enable us to know what he knew." (p.11) Because
such knowledge transcends the changes wrought by the centuries, Barth wanted "to rethink the whole material and to
wrestle with it" until the walls that separate our time
from Paul's "become transparent", and that means "until
a distinction between yesterday and today becomes impossible" (p.7). Most exegetes had quite different objectives, and neither side was ready to yield. When they
accused him of being an enemy of historical criticism,
he accused them of not being critical enough to measure
the words of Paul by the matters about which Paul speaks
(p.68). He believed that scholars who did not put first
what Paul put first were bound to do violence to the
text. To him, the Scriptures released an awe in the
presence of the eternal which relativized most of the
issues which the exegetes considered important. They,
in contrast, encouraged an awe in the presence of history
which led them to downgrade the significance of the
apostle's word from the Lord (p.9). Their obsession with

17

matters of detail induced from Barth the jibe that "in times of spiritual poverty, historical analysis is a method we are bound to adopt" (p.147). Quite apart from the question of its truth, such a sword-thrust does not conciliate opponents.

Typical of an extreme reaction is that of John T. McNeill: "When the philosopher, the theologian and the social theorist leave the stage, it is the historiographer who takes over. Humanly speaking, the last judgment is inscribed on Clio's scroll."[30] Barth could not share in such an evaluation of historiography. "The course of history does not in itself constitute the judgment of history" (p.58). When men assign to historical time the right to preside at the final judgment, time "continually slips away into infinity and is therefore lost forever". Time becomes the "abyss of our non-being".[31] Barth's view of the temporal process was far more favorable than that, since the works of love can redeem time in ways far beyond the historian's knowing. This contrast between McNeill and Barth may serve to summarize the state of the debate in 1922.

During the half century since, the lines of conflict have changed very little. To test this conviction, let us turn to a section of the Church Dogmatics in which Barth dealt directly and fully with the problem of time, in dialogue with three outstanding exegetes. I have in mind the chapter "Man in His Time" in the second part of Volume III. I do not suggest that Barth intended any correlation between Dogmatics and Commentary; nevertheless a comparison of the two will serve to bring out certain variables and constants in Barth's thought.

Many variables are quite obvious. Barth now writes no longer as a pastor but as a professor of theology.[32] His rhetoric is less explosive and more disciplined; his logic is woven more tightly. He explores each issue more patiently and extensively, carefully articulating each conclusion. He places less reliance on vivid images and tantalizing paradoxes, and gives opposing viewpoints the courtesy of more extended rebuttal. Into his argument he draws from both Testaments a wide range of biblical evidence. He often gives more prominence to data from the Gospels than the Epistles, and when he wants to clinch his argument he often selects an apt text from the Apocalypse. (The role of Barth as theologian might more often be compared to that of John the Theologue). There are

also important shifts in vocabulary and categories. He
is, for example, less prone to speak of "the strange new
world" as being unhistorical or nonhistorical. Nor does
he accentuate the distinction between time and eternity,
as if the two worlds were bounded by that distinction.
He is more likely to let the biblical history itself suggest the appropriate temporal categories.

For all these changes, however, we are nonetheless impressed by the degree to which the structural convictions
remain constant. As in the Commentary we find warnings
against the forced harmonizing of biblical thought: "Dogmatics has neither the occasion nor the duty to become a
technical cosmology or a Christian world view" (III/2,p.6).
"There is no world outlook which can be described as biblical, or even as Old Testament or New Testament, or as
prophetic or Pauline" (III/2,p.9). In fact, Barth continued to insist that faith has always been "radically dis-
loyal" to any dominant view of the world (III/2,p.8). He
did not find such disloyalty among the exegetes; they, in
turn, accused him of attributing to the Bible his own har-
monized world view.

He approached his analysis of time as an aspect of anthropology (e.g. "Man lives in his time" p.437); but, of
course, since man is viewed as a creature of God, his
time becomes an aspect of God's activity. "God himself
once took time and thus treated it as something real.
But ... there is no such thing as absolute time, no im-
mutable law of time. ... There is no time in itself,
rivaling God and imposing conditions on him. There is no
god called Chronos. ... As all creation has its goal in
what God purposes and will do and does within it for man,
for us, so time as its historical form has its meaning in
the particular time which God once took for the execution
of his purpose. ... This is the hidden meaning of all
time. ... Time in itself has no property, no laws, to
preclude the control of all other times by this time"
(III/2,p.456). We cannot, therefore, know what time it
is without knowing the will of God. The various times
must be understood theologically.

This conviction that all times are controlled and therefore must be understood in terms of "this time of Deus
praesens" (p.456) Barth considers as a corollary of the
revelation of God in Jesus Christ. This revelation distinguishes and yet unifies the two histories, the two
times of Jesus, one before and one after his resurrection.

Barth believes that we must safeguard the reality of both
and interpret the significance of all other times in terms
of their relation to these two. To say that Jesus is the
Lord of time is to say that "like all other men, the man
Jesus is in his time. ... the time he needs like all other
men to be able to live a human life. ... He not only lives
with God, but for him..not only lives with men but for
them. ... It is this content of his life which makes the
barrier of his time on every side a gateway. ... His time
becomes time for God and therefore for all men...The answer given by the life of Jesus to the questions of God
and man makes his time the time which always was when men
lived, which always is when they live and which always
will be when they will live. It makes this life at once
the centre and the beginning and end of all the times of
all lifetimes of all men...makes him the contemporary of
all men" (III/2,p.439f).
     There is thus in Barth's view a concordance between
Jesus' first history and the history of all other men;
but there is also an even more significant concordance
between Jesus' second history and other histories, since
this second history, the Easter history, reveals and rat-
ifies the first. In dealing with the resurrection, Barth
insists that "we are here in the sphere of history and
time no less than in the case of the words and acts and
even the death of Jesus" (p.442). Easter time is the
time of Jesus, "the time of the revelation of the mystery
of the preceding time of the life and death of the man
Jesus. The two times are inseparably linked" (p.455).
Easter time is also the time of God, the time of "the
appearance and presence of God", "the time of all times
because what God does in it is the goal of all creation
and therefore of all created time" (p.455). "His eternity is authentic temporality and therefore the source
of all time" (p.437). To be sure God "has a different
time from that of men", but in Christ he has disclosed
his decision "to give man a share in this time of his,
in his eternity" (p.451). In Christ's time, God became
temporal, making it clear that "his own time (is) at the
heart of all the times of the being created by him" (p.455).
     In our study of the Commentary we noted how the command-
ment of love became Barth's clue to the eschatological
situation, since the work of love marks the dawning of
the kingdom in both its presentness and its futurity.
When measured by the frequency of the word, the notion of

love is not so prominent in this section of the Dogmatics,
yet the reality is even more pervasive than in the
Commentary. Without reference to grace, the discussion
of "man in his time" becomes empty. It is God's grace
that is embodied in his gift of his eternal time "to the
men of all time". He willed to have time for men "in
order to inaugurate and establish his covenant". Men can
have no share in this authentic temporality, this eternal
time, apart from the time of Jesus, who "represents the
grace of God". The Easter history, which makes Jesus
"absolutely present temporally" conveys on them all the
marks of being in Christ, all the rights of heavenly cit-
izenship (p.467). Because he now rules over their lives,
they receive from him whatever gifts of the Spirit may be
needed (p.468).

The mastery of the times has thus been demonstrated by
God, whose grace relativizes and diversifies all measure-
ments of time. Grace limits and bounds our time, but includes it within his eternal time (p.568). "Death is our
frontier. But our God is the frontier even of our death"
(p.611). Because God is "wholly and utterly for us", his
nearness or distance are not to be measured chronologically
but by the dynamics of grace. Thus Barth leaves no doubt
that he is dealing at every point with the love of God
for men, though he postpones to other sections a detailed
treatment of the commandment of love and its bearing on
Christian ethics (p.633). What seems most clear, when
we compare this section of the Dogmatics with the
Commentary, is the accent upon God's time, eternal time,
the two times of Jesus, as a reality which both limits
and fulfills all other times.

In this same section of the Dogmatics Barth summarizes
the issues on which he differs from his New Testament
colleagues. He makes it clear that in his judgment they
have defaulted on their basic responsibilities: "The time
does not yet seem to have arrived when the dogmatician can
accept with a good conscience and confidence the findings
of his colleagues in Old Testament and New Testament
studies...So long as so many exegetes have not better
learned or practiced their part in this common task; so
long as so many still seem to pride themselves on being
utterly unconcerned as to the dogmatic presuppositions
and consequences of their notions, while unwittingly
reading them into the picture, the dogmatician is forced
to run the same risk as the non-expert and work out his

own proof from Scripture" (III/2/ix). When Barth takes
up specific faults of specific scholars, he stresses their
defective attitudes toward the temporal. Their presuppositions are such as to prevent the Easter faith from
altering in any decisive way their prior conceptions of
time. They agree in recognizing the full temporality of
the history of Jesus in his life-time (p. 440), but
differ in interpreting the temporal dimension of that
"further history" which began on the third day after his
death (p. 441). Let us look at his comments on three
scholars.

Barth takes issue with Kümmel for failing to mention
the resurrection in his book dealing with Promise and
Fulfilment, as if that event were not "the axiom which
controlled all their thinking about this man in His time"
(p. 443).

He launches a sharper attack upon his colleague at
Basel, Oscar Cullmann, especially for his defence of the
thesis that biblical authors attributed to a system of
linear time an independence and an absoluteness which
was unaffected by their experience of the resurrection.
"Surely it was a particular memory of a particular time
filled with a particular history, it was the constraint
under which this laid on their thinking, which formed and
initiated their particular conception of time" (p. 443).
Cullmann's fixed idea of time as a geometrically rigid
ascending line with a successive series of aeons made impossible any thought of contemporaneity "between the
history of Jesus and the prophetic history of Israel".
To counter such a rejection, Barth writes: "Just as the
tradition and recollection of (Jesus) makes Him the contemporary of the Church, so in the time of Israel the
premise and expectation of His coming makes Him the contemporary of Israel. In both cases, it is a spiritual
contemporaneity, perceptible only through him and only in
faith. Where there is no revelation on His part or faith
on ours... the history of Israel will become a history in
which He has not come. The line of time, with its obvious
differentiation of distance and proximity, then acquires...
an absolute significance" (p. 481f.).

It was, however, with Rudolf Bultmann that Barth carried
on his longest and sharpest debate; in this debate most
issues centered on basic attitudes toward time and history.
Bultmann, followed by most exegetes, so defined history as
to deny to the resurrection of Jesus the status of historical

fact. He did not allow to that 'event' any power to alter prior conceptions of the temporal process. He agreed with Barth, of course, in affirming faith in the resurrection, but he located this event "not in time but beyond it". It did not enter the zone of history where it could be dealt with by the historian "as an event in time and space" (p. 444); it could only be confessed by the believer as conveying the meaning of the Cross. To Barth, this dogmatic presupposition regarding the nature of time and history forces exegesis into an "anthropological straitjacket", distorting the entire range of early Christian thinking. He poses three questions for his opponent: 1: "Is it true that an event alleged to have happened in time can be accepted as historical only if it can be proved to be a 'historical' fact in Bultmann's sense -- i.e., when it is open to verification by the methods and, above all, by the tacit assumptions, of modern historical scholarship?" 2: "Is it true that the assertion of the historicity of an event which by its very nature is inaccessible to 'historical' verification ... is merely a blind acceptance of a piece of mythology, an arbitrary act, a descent from faith to works?" 3: "Is it true that modern thought is 'shaped for good or ill by modern science' ... (and that) this modern view (is) so binding as to determine in advance and unconditionally our acceptance or rejection of the biblical message?" (pp. 446f.).

Having now summarized the debate thirty years after the Commentary, what may we say about the prospect of a resolution of the issues outstanding in 1972 between Barth and the exegetes? It seems to me that the chasm is no less wide in 1972 than it was in 1922. Various exegetes have taken various initiatives to move beyond Bultmann, but none of these initiatives has basically challenged the dominance of Bultmann's conception of time and history. None has proposed any significant modification in the assumptions and methods of historical scholarship. There are exceptions, of course; but none of these individual scholars has attracted any substantial following. Among American exegetes, B.S. Childs mentions only Otto Piper and myself;[33] among British scholars we might mention E. Hoskyns and J. Marsh. Quite typical is the silence about Barth in a recent series of essays on The Significance of the Message of the Resurrection for Faith in Jesus Christ.[34] Of the three New Testament

scholars who deal with this theme, none of them so much as
mentions Barth. Moreover, in the leading article W.
Marxsen demands an absolute separation between the historical and the theological approaches to the resurrection.
He insists that as a historian no scholar can make any
judgment about the resurrection as a historical fact.
"Historical perception (i.e., historical exegesis) can
always only state that witnesses claimed to have encoun-
tered God in Jesus" (p.21).

This unanimity in rejecting Barth is all the more surprising when we consider developments in other sectors.
I have in mind such matters as these: the widespread
influence of Barth in other disciplines; the growing
disaffection with scientific methodologies as providing
acceptable models for historical reconstruction;[35] the
application to theological language of the insights of
contemporary linguistics; the recent discoveries concerning time-consciousness on the part of novelists,
dramatists and literary critics.[36] Exegetes are not
noted, however, for their knowledge of what is happening
in other disciplines; they are more likely to seek the
plaudits of contemporary secular historians, even though
this may mean endorsing assumptions which are no longer
applied by the ablest of them. The cumulative effects of
these and other developments may in the future produce a
change in the patterns of biblical exegesis, but the
changes which are visible today seem strangely devoid of
Barthian influence. Rare indeed is any reference to the
potential contributions of the Commentary to an understanding
of Paul (e.g., in his own Commentary on Romans, C.K.
Barrett gratefully acknowledges a vast debt to Barth for
Christian faith but this indebtedness does not often ex-
tend to Barrett's understanding of Romans). It is not often
that one can find among New Testament scholars any reference to the massive exegetical fine-print of the
Dogmatics. We do not, of course, expect an imitation of
Barth's style or easy agreement with his conclusions, but
we expect a renewed effort to cope with those realities
which Barth has shown were the prime concern of biblical
authors. That kind of effort is no more visible today
than it was in German biblical scholarship during the
First World War. Historiography is no more capable of
dealing with "the strange new world" than it was before
its discovery by Barth and Thurneysen.

I do not wish, however, to end on a note of despondency.

The continuing impasse between Barth and the exegetes is
simply an urgent invitation to examine the reasons for it.
I believe that one reason lies in the choice of the major
categories for dealing with the various realities under
review. Both sides have adopted such terms as time,
history, world, beginning and end, as if those terms had
a common content on which both sides could agree. These
terms, however, have lost their precision and therefore
their usefulness. When used in discussion, their meanings
shift so secretly and so subtly that mutual understanding
is prevented rather than enhanced. So when Barth speaks
of Easter time or eternal time, the categories themselves
become obstacles to comprehension. Yet none of these
categories is genuinely biblical, and no biblical category is roughly equivalent to them. There is urgent need
to locate within the Bible an alternative vocabulary which
can deal with the same realities without entailing the
same difficulties.
     For instance, in dealing with the relation of time and
eternity (a relation which lies outside the zone of
reality which historical methodology was designed to
cope with), we would be wise to recover and refurbish
the ontological categories of heaven and earth which are
so pervasive in the Bible. Bultmann has done exegesis
a great disservice by trivializing the biblical heaven,
as if it were solely a mark of an outmoded cosmology,
whereas it is frequently used as an effective cosmological
metaphor to serve ontological and hermeneutical functions.
Barth was more alert to recognize and to specify those
functions. He recognized that when a biblical author
speaks of heaven he often is thinking of a "time which
is beyond time, space which has no locality" (Commentary,
p.92). Heaven is indubitably real as "the sphere from
which God speaks and acts toward man" (Dogmatics
III/2/16). Or, as he writes in a later volume, "to say
God in the biblical sense ... is also to say heaven"
(III/3/419). The term functions as a pointer to "the
divine horizon of human life", "the sum of the created
reality which is invisible, unknown and inaccessible to
man" (III/2/11; also III/3/424), "the sum of that which
is really invisible or invisibly real" (III/3/425).
These assertions strike near the mark of biblical modes
of thinking.37
     Yet in spite of its viability Barth forgoes any further
use of this category and prefers the controverted terms

time, history, eternity. Moreover, he uses these latter
terms in ways which are bound to increase both baffle-
ment and resistance. He seems to relish such paradoxical
phrases as this: "the non-historical factor which is the
beginning and end of history" (Commentary, p. 146). This,
too, has done a disservice to exegesis by turning attention away from the reality itself to the language of the
commentator. Bultmann's concept of historical time has
proved too limited to do justice to those realities which
Barth discerned "behind Paul" (III/3/375); Barth's concept has been too complex, too mysterious, too inclusive,
to clarify thought or convey conviction. The complexi-
ties and the mysteries might, I think, be better conveyed
by a more discriminating reference to those events in
heaven which precede, correspond to and follow related
events on earth. "Easter time" is a category which can
hardly be assimilated into historical methods; the New
Testament message concerning the continued heavenly activities of the Enthroned Lord creates difficulties; but
I believe that here the difficulties are less insuper-
able. To be sure, the New Testament agrees with Isaiah
that God's people requires a prophet to serve as its eyes
(29:10), to see and to tell what is happening in heaven.
But, given this prophetic vision, heavenly realities can
become the basis of earthly life. Both Barth and Bultmann
have, I think, underestimated the viability of the term
heaven and the continued necessity of the role of the
prophet as a revealer of heavenly realities. Barth tacitly
expects the historian to fulfill the prophet's vocation;
Bultmann is sure that no historian as a historian should
attempt it. Post-Bultmannian exegetes are currently ob-
sessed with the creative power of language. If they could
supplement their often profound insight into language
events with an equally profound awareness of the ontological reality of heaven and an adequate recognition of
the work of the prophetic interpreters of heavenly events,
they might be able to do greater justice to Barth's concept of eternal time. What continues to play havoc with
the lines of communication between Barth and his exegetical colleagues is the fact that the Scriptures, which
convey the prophetic disclosure of heavenly realities to
the churches, have become the exclusive jurisdiction of
professional scholars, whose vocabularies and methodologies
have been created by secular disciplines to serve quite
alien functions. We cannot expect any major change in

this respect until Christian scholars mount their own
liberation movement.

Relevant in this connection is a bit of humorous verse
which in 1926 Barth considered the best review of Der
Roemerbrief:

> "God needs men, not creatures
> Full of noisy, catchy phrases,
> Dogs he asks for, who their noses
> Deeply thrust into -- Today,
> And there scent Eternity.
>
> Should it lie too deply buried,
> Then go on, and fiercely burrow,
> Excavate until -- Tomorrow." (Commentary, p.24)

Barth viewed himself as such a dog, a dog of the Lord,
who deplored the reluctance of his exegetical colleagues
to burrow more fiercely into the Scriptures where he
scented Eternity. On their part, his colleagues have
found it virtually impossible to accept this burrowing
as an essential part of their vocation.

Let me close by telling one of my most vivid memories
of Karl Barth. During the years 1951 - 1953 he worked as
a member of an advisory commission producing a working
paper to be used at the Second Assembly of the World
Council of Churches. We were meeting in Switzerland in
1953, giving final shape to a document on the theme
"Christ the Hope of the World". After tumultuous and
often acerbated debate, we had approved a final draft of
three substantive sections. On the last evening we became convinced that a fourth concluding section would be
needed. However, we were too exhausted to discuss in detail what it should say; so in desperation we turned to
our most illustrious member, asking him to produce by the
following morning a draft which could serve as basis for
discussion. With a twinkle in his tired eyes he consented.
The next morning he presented us with a draft under the
heading "The Sum of the Matter". This draft was so simple,
so lucid, so comprehensive, so representative, so cogent,
that with very few amendments the Commission adopted it -
a very rare thing in the life of such commissions. Some
of the sentences in that draft apply not only to that
single document but to all Barth's writing as well:

"It is a human witness to a thing that is itself divine.
We are well aware of the poverty and obscurity of our

expression of it. ... Among the earthly hopes of which
we have spoken we must also place this one - that it
may be given to those who come after us, in saying
again the self-same thing, to say it differently, more
clearly and more truly. And beyond that we await the
eternal light which will at last illumine the darkness
that besets even the best thoughts and words of sinful
men."[38]

NOTES

1   The Epistle to the Romans, London, Oxford University
    Press, 1933, p. VI, tr. E. Hoskyns
2   The Word of God and the Word of Man, Grand Rapids,
    Zondervan, 1935, p. 100, tr. D. Horton
3   cf. Childs, op. cit., ch. 1
4   T.H.L. Parker, Karl Barth, Grand Rapids, Eerdmans,
    p. 16
5   Smart, Revolutionary Theology in the Making, Richmond,
    John Knox Press, 1964, p. 34
6   The Word of God and the Word of Man, p. 22
7   The Humanity of God, Richmond, John Knox Press, 1960,
    p. 14
8   Parker, op. cit., p. 19
9   The Word of God and the Word of Man, p. 100
10 Smart, op. cit., p. 75
11 For an influential statement of the "two-desk" posi-
    tion, cf. K. Stendahl, Interpreter's Dictionary of
    the Bible, New York, Abingdon, 1962, vol. I, p.420f.
12 Smart, op. cit., p. 48
13 "The Righteousness of God", "The Strange New World in
    the Bible", "Biblical Questions, Insights and Vistas",
    published in The Word of God and the Word of Man.
14 The Word of God and the Word of Man, p. 60
15 Ibid., p. 60, Barth's italics.
16 Ibid., p. 60
17 Ibid., p. 9
18 Ibid., p. 9
19 Ibid., p. 26
20 Ibid., p. 62
21 Smart, op. cit., p. 32
22 Ibid., p. 43
23 The Word of God and the Word of Man, p. 66

28

24 Ibid., p. 72
25 Eyes of Faith, Philadelphia, Westminster, 1946, p. 5
26 The Word of God and the Word of Man, p. 37
27 Parker, op. cit., p. 33
28 cf. Kerygma and Myth, London, SPCK, 1953, pp. 1-44,
    tr. R. Fuller
29 cf. S. Kierkegaard, Works of Love, Princeton, 1946,
    pp. 201-213.
30 Religion in Life, vol. 22, 1953, p. 586
31 Church Dogmatics, III/2, p. 521
32 The Epistle to the Romans, p. 23
33 Op. cit., p. 42f
34 ed. by C.F.D. Moule, London, SCM, 1968
35 cf. T.S. Kuhn, The Structure of Scientific Revolutions,
    Chicago, 1962
36 e.g. G. Poulet, Studies in Human Time, New York,
    Harper, 1956; A.A. Mendilov, Time and the Novel,
    London, Neville, 1952
37 A rare instance of exegetical indebtedness to Barth
    may be found in the essay on ouranos by H. Traub in
    Kittel, Theological Dictionary of the New Testament,
    tr. by G.W. Bromiley, vol. V. Traub relies extensively
    on Barth's treatment of heaven (III/3, p.369-531) and
    insists, against Bultmann, that this term at no point
    in the New Testament loses its symbolic character
    (V, 514). Rather it serves as an essential "inte-
    grating focus for the present and future blessings
    of salvation in the new aeon" (V, 532)
38 Christ - the Hope of the World. Documents on the
    Main Theme. Geneva, World Council of Churches, 1954,
    p. 39

JOSEPH C. McLELLAND

This essay is absolutely elusive (cf. my note, 5,)
But there is a sum on
pg. 47.

Philosophy and Theology - A Family Affair
(Karl and Heinrich Barth)

Karl Barth once wrote an essay in honor of his brother
Heinrich, entitled simply <u>Philosophie und Theologie</u>.[1]
His thesis is typically bold and engaging: "The opposition
between 'Philosophy' and 'Theology' is (to mythologize a
little) an Abstraction. What they truly have in common
is the encounter of determinate <u>men</u> of diverse interests,
commitments and engagements: the opposition and the asso-
ciation of Philosopher and Theologian". After a development of this thesis, Barth the theologian says to Barth
the philosopher: "And if they are not only fellow-creatures
(<u>Mitmenschen</u>), but wishing more earnestly on both sides
to be Christian, then despite this last mutual reservation,
it may be possible for them to behave according to the
intention of Psalm 133:1. The Father of the <u>Jubilar</u> - to
whom this book and therefore also this essay is dedicated
- and of myself, used to call to us on certain occasions
in our younger days, with finger raised: 'See, how good
and lovely it is when brothers live together in harmony!'"[2]
    That thesis and that insight from Karl Barth's mature
years (he was 74 and Heinrich was 70; the year was 1960)
provide the orientation for this paper. I will <u>not</u> attempt the impossible dream of showing that Barth was
"really" open to philosophy, that he operated with a
consistent view of the relation between philosophy and
theology, or that he appreciated the philosophical options
which his own theology implied. In short, I find myself
in constant disagreement with Barth's position on these
issues, despite my sympathy with his essential teaching.
Or perhaps it were better to say: <u>because</u> of my indebtedness to him, I am free to engage him in debate! For he
would indeed appreciate the irony of a Barthian "philosopher of religion".
    There are too many questions in this area even to touch
upon in one paper. Many of them seem strangely neglected
(so far as I know) in the already vast Barthian secondary
literature. Here are some questions that appear important
for my present <u>essai</u>. How far is the early Barth, including the "earliest" Barth at Neo-Kantian Marburg
(along with his brother Heinrich), determinative for the

later, despite the apparently dramatic shifts from the
first <u>Romans</u> to the second, and the first <u>Dogmatics</u> to
the second? What was Heinrich's influence at the formative stage, in interpreting Plato and Kant, in showing
the way to a philosophy of appearance and event, and in
reinforcing certain epistemological approaches that dom-
inate the <u>Dogmatik</u>'s view of thought and language? Are
the two brothers to be regarded as complementary, as
Karl's tribute to Heinrich suggests? If so, is Heinrich
perhaps the silent partner, the hidden philosophical
agenda behind much of Karl's vaunted "non-philosophical"
assumptions? Or is it a case of Heinrich's being bound
to theological premises as Karl is to philosophical?

Such questions remind us of the scope of any enquiry
into Barth: and since he has claimed to be offering "an
alternative to the <u>mixophilosophico-theologia</u>"[3] of modern
thought, it is especially difficult to charge <u>him</u> with
concocting such a mixture, however small be the philosophical ingredients, or however subconscious the recipe.
In order to make my point I shall present sections on the
transcendentalist <u>problématique</u>, the transitional research
leading to the book on Anselm, and the constant aim of
purifying theology as a scientific project.

(1) PROBLEMATIQUE: THE TRANSCENDENTALIST STANCE

The story of what Barth would later call "my trapeze
work" as a neophyte theologian shows us how he and Heinrich
learned about history from their father Fritz and attended
Marburg where Cohen and Natorp were developing their distinctive kind of neo-Kantianism; and how Karl as pastor
and professor struggled with his gigantic homework (scriptures, fathers, doctors, the newspaper) until he astonished
the theological world with his <u>Römerbrief</u> of 1918. This
early period has been examined almost <u>ad nauseam</u>, yet it
remains one of the clues to Barth's position. He himself
once remarked in a letter to Thurneysen that he had re-
luctantly come to see Luther's superiority over Zwingli
on the doctrine of the Supper, "specifically in the study
of the <u>earlier</u> writings of Luther, where one can see it as
it <u>comes into being</u>".[4] Similarly, I suggest that Barth's
relationship to the Kantian problematics remains a decisive orientation throughout his career. Kant's question
was, How are synthetic <u>a priori</u> judgments possible? His
aim was to provide a rational foundation for science,

31

despite the radical scepticism of Hume. His answer was
to articulate the "transcendental unity of apperception"
and to lay bare, through his critical Triplizität, the
inherent rationality of human judgment in the face of
truth, goodness and beauty.

There is a popular image of the early Barth as one who
began with a Platonic-Kantian stance (I Romans), moved
through a Kierkegaardian phase (2 Romans) and issued in
a third and final stage thanks to the discovery of
Anselmic method: Henri Bouillard has summarized the thesis
well, and even Barth himself seems to have accepted it.[5]
My counter-thesis is that the Platonic-Kantian base provides a constant, a permanent element in Barth's thought.
For one thing, it presented him with the well-established
anti-metaphysical tradition of Germany. If Ritschl is
the name associated with this view, it was Herrmann, whom
Barth called "the teacher of my student years", whose
critique of rational orthodoxy involved a strategic and
direct attack on metaphysics, which he considered a mis-
taken attempt to solve the ethical question posed by
Kant.[6] Kant had driven reason beyond the antinomies of
its pure scientific form, to achieve contact with Truth
through a kind of moral positivism. The problematics of
the Kantian system are grasped identically by the early
Barth and the early Brunner, as they took up the debate
with philosophical realism and idealism.[7] Both insisted
that one must begin with a critique of reason, a mapping
of its limited powers, and then must proceed to describe
the rationality of an autonomous area of special knowledge.
It is this general agreement with Kantian method that
lends weight to the similar charge of at least one friend
(Bonhoeffer) and one foe (Van Til), who claim that Barth
is Kantian. Facing an unknowable realm of being, transcendental method accepts the dialectical response of the
subject as the dynamic of epistemology, Bonhoeffer saw
Barth's radical contingency of Act and Word as rendering
"unequivocal theological statements" impossible, so that
his dialectical theology paralleled Kant's "critical reservation".[8] His later charge of "revelation positivism"
seems a logical development of this thesis, which we shall
examine below.

Meanwhile, the question is, did Barth remain in the
transcendentalist stance, the philosophical theory that
man knows his world through a subjective act of unifying
appropriation, and therefore speaks of this knowledge

through a language of dialectic? Is his intellectual
pilgrimage, like that of his brother, a way from Kant
through Kierkegaard to a more critical idealism? For
Heinrich begins with a Philosophy of Practical Reason,
1927, which shows evidence of dialogue with the new
Existenzphilosophie. He also displays similar interests
to Karl: freedom in Augustine's thought, philosophy of
existence, and at last his major work on philosophy of
appearance.[9] Let us reserve judgment on these Kantian-
sounding signs, while remarking the striking unity of
the brothers in their respective disciplines.

Kierkegaard has been mentioned: one fears and trembles
to do more, for here the battle is indeed joined. Barth
himself has stated that S.K. is someone through whose
school one must pass; and one must pass. In his own
"egg-shell" period symbolized by 2 Römerbrief he was able
to execute a "turn of 180 degrees" thanks to the Danish
catalyst.[10] Barth claimed to have remained "faithful to
Kierkegaard's reveille" which continued to sound like "a
strong accompaniment (Unterton) next to others". Yet he
scored the negative mood of such training in Christianity,
and especially the Heils-individualismus that could offer
foundation for a philosophy of existence and even a theology of subjectivity.[11] The "Dank und Reverenz" which he
owed Kierkegaard is thus charged to a definite period, a
transition, when he was just the thing, the pinch of spice,
to introduce a critique of idealism. Now the difficulty
lies here, in the image Barth holds of S.K. and the subsequent image of Barth to be implied. Kierkegaard is
taken as a type of irrationalist, helpful as therapy (after
all, he called himself "a laxative"), stressing the notorious diastasis, the break, the "infinite qualitative distinction" and All That; but not much good on the positive
side, the side of subsequent rationality, the constructive
theology to which Barth was heading.

Alistair McKinnon charges that this is the image of a
"phantom" S.K., the result of misunderstanding the intention
of his pseudonymous utterances. The "real" Kierkegaard
emerges through recognizing the authorship and the moving
figure behind it. To grapple with the Kierkegaardian
tour de force, argues McKinnon, is to drop the charge of
irrationality and focus on paradox, and to identify the
very stages or process which characterizes Barth himself.
Therefore he can state: "At least in respect of the present
crucial question, the position of the early Barth is identical

33

with that of the phantom Kierkegaard. Similarly, the
position of the mature Barth is identical with that of
the real Kierkegaard".[12] This view is part of an apologia
for the authentic Kierkegaardian voice; but it suggests
"something about Barth" along the way. It suggests that
he, too, began with the negative print, the inauthentic
speech of diastasis, of those Kantian antinomies which
break the ground to receive the positivistic seed; and
[that he, too, shifted not only to the positive pole but
to an alternative understanding of the "rationality" of
faith, beyond the paradox.] If this is so, Barth is not
- in his mature period at least - properly described as
dialectical, as moving within a polarity of negative and
positive; but rather he is one who [renounces this earlier
and Kantian substructure for a new base.] I think McKinnon
is correct about Kierkegaard; I am still doubtful about
Barth.

[margin: - crit of this view of Barth:]
[margin: viz: THESIS is: NO SUCH CHANGE]
[margin: - with this view of SK.]

(2) TRANSITUS - ANALYTIC A POSTERIORI JUDGMENTS

The key to our thesis rests with those transitional
years from 2 Romans to 2 Dogmatics. Two texts seem
crucial for our purpose: the Dortmund lectures of 1929
(Schicksal und Idee in der Theologie), and the book on
Anselm of 1931. Let me propose a query: If Kant's philosophical question is, How are synthetic a priori judgments
possible? is Barth's theological question, "How are analytic a posteriori judgments possible?" For it seems clear
from his work on Anselmic method that he came to see how
theology is able (i.e., how it is possible) to make analytic judgments concerning the God who is revealed "in
some other way".

[margin: 1 - DORT. MUND.]

The Dortmund lectures suggest Barth's initial research,
forced by many pressures upon him after the dramatic shift
of 2 Romans. The implications of his break with Harnack
were becoming clearer, as Martin Rumscheidt's work displays.[13] The concept of subjectivity, clarified by the
Kierkegaard study, had to be thought through in dialogue
with Schleiermacher - I think that the significance of
Brunner's Die Mystik und das Wort in this regard might
prove considerable, especially for Barth's own later reflections on Religion in its mystical dimension: "mysticism
is esoteric atheism"![14] It was at this point that Barth
sought to clarify his relation to philosophy, or rather
to certain philosophical issues of epistemology or

34

objectivity. T.F. Torrance is particularly helpful in
examining this period. He thinks that "The really decisive transition in Barth's thinking took place about
1930"; that it had to do with "the prior understanding
of man bound up with a general anthropology"; and that
"Barth swept aside all remnants of the language of idealist philosophy, even of Kierkegaard and particularly of
the existentialist misunderstanding of Kierkegaard".[15]

Philosophy has halted between two opinions: the objectivity of Schicksal and the subjectivity of Idee. The
first concept involves the question of what is real
(Wirklichkeit)[16] and the second of what is true (Wahrheit)[17].
Thus Realism and Idealism emerge as Barth's subject-matter.
Here is the overlap of philosophy and theology, in this
dilemma of object and thought, one horn of which represents
heteronomy and the other, autonomy. For the reality of
object suggests that God is "ontologically and noetically
man's Destiny". An uncritical stress on the statement
"God is" leads to an objectivity which posits a necessary
relationship between beings and Being, a heteronomous relationship that binds us velite nolite to God as Fate.
Such analogia entis, however, misses the "critical realism"
(if we may term it) which the Gospel introduces by its
announcement that the Word took flesh. For now a modality
of presence is revealed - presents itself - in which the
Other moves towards us as a Thou. Yes, the Ich und Du
terminology is explicit here, and another motif begs examination, the significance of the "Patmos group" with
their vocabulary of Logos, of I-Thou encounter, of the
reverberating Word.[18] For Barth, the Gospel represents
the unexpected, the surprising news that our race towards
Necessity has been interrupted from "outside" - and in
such a way that the very "inside" of our subjective apprehension of that Act is itself part of this new reality.
The natural and the necessary, matched by our knowledge
and our acceptance - the realist dynamics of all that
world of philosophy are challenged by Barth's theological
analysis. Revelation here presents a new possibility, a
God known not in his static inevitability but in his
motion toward man, in seinem Kommen. This last point distinguishes the living God from Nature - and from Demons!

Idealism replaces the choice of heteronomy with one of
autonomy. Distrusting naive realism, it places confidence
in the act of knowing, in spirit. The sinister connection
between idealist philosophy and mysticism is noted, along

35

with the further implication that this very connection
warns us against simplistic reductionism, as if types
of philosophy lead to only one theology. That is, for
Barth there are parallels between philosophy and theology
rather than logical connections. Both realism and idealism guarantee authentic elements in the structure of human
knowledge, so that theology must always learn their lessons.
Realism warns us not to forget the givenness of the object;
idealism reminds us that the object is given to us, to
human minds. This is not, for Barth, so much a polarization
(as it was for Kant's response to the realism of Hume and
the idealism of Descartes, for example) as it is a mutual
critique, each one engaging in constant criticism of the
other. Therefore here, Barth seems to reject Kantianism
in a fundamental way, to deny the synthesis of the German
tradition on behalf of genuine dialectic. If realism
raised the spectre of Demonism, idealism raises another
across the way - Ideology. For in accepting the idealist
warning, theology may be tempted (Barth mentions A. Ritschl
explicitly) to develop its abstracted thinking, its subjective logos, die Welt des Geistes, into the way to God.
Barth grants Schleiermacher the mastery in this point at
least, that he knew that "God is to be sought above these
inner-worldly oppositions".

Barth's epistemology is already clear. He sees the
human mind involved in both "spontaneity and receptivity",
an antithesis which theology cannot escape. The question,
however, is whether theology will be content to accept both
sides of its dialectic from God, against certain idealist
definitions of the power of discursive reason. Barth insists that theology is "science", but not simply one of
the "human sciences" (Wissenschaft, Geisteswissenschaften).
For its "object" is not a thing, to which the entire an-
tithetical structure of reason applies; its "object" moves
towards this structure from above it, rendering this entire "tension" (Spannung) responsible to a new structure,
The new, theological, structure was described by the
Reformers as "passive". It represents, for Barth, an
"other" knowledge, which he describes as ac-knowledgement
(An-Erkenntnis).

In the third section of the Dortmund lectures,[19] Barth
reflects on the philosophy-theology relationship. Both
occupy the same field, operate by the same dialectical
movement, grapple with actuality and truth. But philosophy
tries to have the whole say, to develop a synthesis that

will "solve" the problem. Against such an anthropology
or even theosophy, theology opposes its witness to revelation. There is a contradiction to be expected as the
Word of God confronts the structure of human knowledge,
but it will be a different <u>kind</u> of contradiction from
that of the epistemological antitheses described. The
vaunted "synthetic art of philosophy" (<u>die synthetische
Kunst der Philosophie</u>) will not "solve" it. Therefore
where we find a self-limited philosophy at work, one that
describes and interprets the "actuality and truth" of man's
knowledge without turning itself into something more,
there we may find theology at work as partner, in a peace-
ful coexistence.

Here is Barth's dilemma - still the Kantian problematics
to be sure: he wishes "philosophy" to be defined as <u>ancilla
theologiae</u>, a critical and limited exercise in epistemology
whose synthetic art will remain tentative and penultimate.
Insofar as it does so, theology may use it cheerfully. But
how can Barth seriously ask this of philosophy? Only if
he already assumes (subconsciously?) that the philosopher
grants the theological claim and therefore <u>defines</u> philosophy in terms of the theological answer. Only if he already
accepts theology's estimate of a Word of God beyond the
human antithesis can he understand his task as restricted
and partial. And here lies the weakness of Barth's position. He is saying that the only good philosopher is a
Christian philosopher. He is defining philosophy as analytic rather than synthetic, capable of descriptive metaphysics but not of any sort of normative or fundamental
ontology. Indeed, only a Christian - only a Christian of
the Reformed Church! - could pass as philosopher in
Barth's definition. We think of Pierre Thévenaz or Paul
Ricoeur, both of whom would accept such a role for philosophy, I believe. But how is one to meet those philosophers who continue their synthetic work "as if God does
not exist"? It is significant that Barth draws his
Dortmund lectures to a close by examining the role of
theology, and appealing to the doctrine of divine election
as the final criterion of the true ideas of God. I doubt
whether such eschatological verification is viable in the
apologetic realm of debate with philosophers. I grant
that there is considerable evidence that Barth himself
was able to gain a respectful hearing from philosophers,
humanists and scientists by his straightforward declaration of intention in his dogmatic work. But philosophers

37

who claim the freedom to pursue their synthetic task into
concepts of man, of his religion, and of the object of
his religion, will protest against the Barthian definition
of their limits. As responsible philosophers they will
accept no prior limitation upon their analysis of actuality and truth, least of all in the name of some alien
Word which is poised somewhere above human structures.
Not that this is a new problem, or one peculiar to Barth.
But the dilemma seems clear: either philosophy itself
will lead to conversion (ex opere operato), or else the
only philosophical errors are the result of sin.

2 - Anselm
book

Barth's book on Anselm underlines the dilemma. Through
his masterful analysis of Anselm, especially of the threefold ratio and the consequent path (Weg) for theology to
follow,[20] he uncovers the similarity and difference between philosophy and theology. Both are involved with
"truth in the second or middle circle", that is inter-
posed between Truth in the ultimate sense and the human
appropriation of its given form. There is a splendid
sensitivity to Anselm's intention - Barth is one of the
very few commentators to acknowledge that this is theology
in the form of prayer, and not a textbook for introductory
philosophy classes. The remoto Christo is understood
therefore as a strategic shift, a deliberate device to
unpack the logic of the revealed truth. But the analysis
does not and cannot gainsay the revelation, the inter-
position from the side of ultimate Truth. So Barth's
"analytic a posteriori" as I have termed it, is clearly
on display in this work. Revelation creates a situation
in which theological analytic shows how the actual is
possible (indeed, "necessary"), but is not itself analysing
the "other" revelation, "of God in his world", or "on
other grounds".[21]

Barth is quite right to underline Anselm's intention,
namely that the "existence of God" refers to a unique
and peculiar kind. As the sole existence that is both
ultimate and the cause of all other existence, it is "the
only existence which in the strict sense can be proved";
by analysis it is proved also to be necessary, since
"only the finite can be conceived as non-existing".[22] For
our purposes it is not Barth's significant contribution
to the long debate on the Ontological Argument that is
important, but his adoption of the Anselmic method as
that which honors the distinctive theo-logic of revelation.
In this sense, he seeks to answer the Kantian problematic

by positing a second transcendence, beyond the entire
human polarities and antitheses; and by ascribing to this
Transcendent a synthetic art of its own, which embraces
both poles, thesis and antithesis, in its reconciling arms.

A third text from this transitional period supports this
view - the lectures on the Holy Spirit given at Elberfeld
in 1929, along with a companion lecture by Heinrich.[23]
Polemical and sometimes pedantic, the lectures show the
greatest insistence on the all-encompassing role of Holy
Ghost - Creator, Reconciler, Redeemer. The key concept
is that every aspect of our hearing of the Word of God is
God's own work - the familiar Barthian stance is consistent and unrelenting: any hearing we might call our own
would be "only the echo of our own voice, in unbounded
solitariness".[24] This statement occurs in the context of
a discussion of sanctification; it foreshadows the elab-
oration of that doctrine that will occur in the Dogmatics,
where again the point is driven home - even our "participation" in Christ's proper holiness is his work.

What is really at issue here? Who is the enemy that
Barth so carefully hems in on both sides? Why does he
differ so markedly from Tillich, who can write expansively
of man's participation and mean it in its classic sense
of ontological sharing, so similar to the Byzantine meaning? Indeed, is this latter perhaps a key, that Barth is
terribly Western, Augustinian and that is what saddles him
with the Kantian problématique? That is, is he so committed to a theoretical man-as-sinner that he must surrender
every human philosophical epistemology and ontology to the
mark of Cain? We know that his good humour proves ir-
repressible, that he is much better than his theory, that
he is at home with "natural" man. That is an irony that
he perhaps appreciated, but was never able to articulate
within his system.

Here is where the work of Heinrich Barth may assist us.
Like Karl, he began in that Marburg kind of Neo-Kantianism
which may be summed up somewhat like this: a synthesis of
Plato and Kant; acceptance of a critical method in philosophy; a stress on praxis, or applied philosophy; the up-
dating of Kant in light of new mathematics and physics; a
conviction that philosophy must obey Kant's own method
and spirit, reject speculation and follow "the fact of
science". Cohen and Natorp found themselves battling a
new psychologism, and wedded their idealistic epistemology
to the process of science, particularly the emerging

relativity theories. In part because of the fatal fact/
value dichotomy of modern thought, they appealed to an
immanentist idea of God to function as guarantor of values
(focus imaginarius). One can appreciate Herrmann's similar emphasis on praxis rather than speculation, and reliance on a quasi-positivism of revelation; even Vaihinger's
Kantian als ob theory fits well into this general approach,
while Cassirer (Cohen's pupil) sought for creative sources
in the category of das Symbolische.

Heinrich Barth's own work links up with this, as attested by Karl in the Foreword to 2 Romans: "the better
understanding of the real orientation of the ideas of
Plato and Kant for which I am indebted to the writings of
my brother, Heinrich Barth". His philosophical position
moved towards Existenzphilosophie about the same time
that Karl heard Kierkegaard's reveille. Indeed, Gerhard
Huber's survey of his thought distinguishes three similar
phases to Karl's: ①the initial critical idealism reflecting
Marburg school orientation, ②the transitional encounter
with concepts of freedom and subjectivity issuing in a
form of Existenzphilosophie, ③and a mature reflection on
the concept of appearance (Erscheinung).[25] His writings
on Plato's Lebensphilosphie and Kant's subjective consciousness converged towards a dynamic transcendentalism,
a formal-transzendentalen Idee as Aktfolge, source of
uniting power. He draws together existence and knowledge
(Existieren bedeutet Erkennen), but knowledge in turn
means to follow appearances (Existieren bedeutet In-die-
Erscheinung-Treten).[26] The concept of appearance or
phenomenon moves to centre stage, as he develops a cluster
of themes, notably the appearance as event and therefore
in tension with Idea: "Philosophical knowledge sees itself
therefore as called on to see through appearances to the
idea (Eidos) that dwells within it, yet without surrender-
ing itself again".[27]

The Philosophie der Erscheinung is a Problemgeschichte,
spanning the centuries from Socrates to Hegel, and attend-
ing to Being and Appearance as ontische Gegenpole. The
first volume (1947) traces the story to the end of the
middle ages, when the primary problem was that of contingency, the form which the appearance-problem was taking.[28]
The second volume (1959) - dedicated to the memory of Paul
Natorp - hails philosophy of appearance as "the open
window of philosophical knowledge". Noting the shift from
the Renaissance "magical consciousness" to the new

40

"mathematical" outlook of modern science, Heinrich Barth
applauds the demise of the Platonic Apriorismus. Critical
of the Cartesian reduction of being to selfhood, he provides in fact a history of philosophy, culminating in
Kant's philosophy of Aesthetics. As a good Neo-Kantian,
and therefore unlike our Anglophone approach to Kant, he
sees the cruciality of the third Critique, where the
facultas imaginandi comes into its own: both productive
and reproductive, mediating between sense and understanding.[29] His conclusion is that philosophy of appearance
opens on to philosophy of Urgrund, as Plato and Kant
understood: from contingency of existence to revelation
of being.

Gerhard Huber's analysis of Heinrich Barth's philosophy
includes a valuable section on knowledge through faith
in relation to philosophy and theology.[30] He notes Barth's
insistence that the range of philosophical reflection must
include the Christian truth, which offers a specific content to the philosopher. At the same time, faith agrees
only with a limited or self-critical philosophy; and this
is what the Kantian transcendental philosophy claims to be.
Its stress on "mere humanity" leaves room for a grounding
in God. There is thus a superiority of the knowledge
through faith (eindeutiger Vorrang der Glaubenserkenntnis),
deriving from the sheer weight of the Word of God. Because of this dimensional difference, no logical category
can subsume both, which remain incommensurable. Philosophical knowledge is at best an "analogy of knowledge of
God".

Here would seem to be a philosophical position in large
accord with Karl Barth's views. It is a limited and
critical philosophy, taking the category of freedom most
seriously, and reserving strict causality to the positive
sciences. Human freedom is the inverse of transcendental
freedom, which may be geared into a doctrine of divine
grace.[31] Heinrich also appears to agree with Karl that
theology is "scientific" in nature, a reflex action set
in motion by a specific sort of appearance, demanding an
appropriate logical enquiry. There is, further, a self-
criticism of the philosopher who recognizes in the diastasis between being and appearance, idea and reality, an
irrevocable structure from the human side.// And yet ...
a trouble remains. Why does Karl deal so gently with
Heinrich - especially in contrast to his harsh treatment
of Brunner? Here is no Nein!, nor even a direct critique

41

of Heinrich's quest for some Urgrund that may or may not
be the Good, or God, or Nothingness. Is it a question of
giving the benefit of the doubt, or is there some "family
matter" hidden here? I do not know.

(3) TELOS: "THE MOST BEAUTIFUL OF ALL SCIENCES"[32]

Kant's ultimate question was: how is a science of metaphysics possible? Barth's is: How is a science of theology possible? And his answer becomes clear during the
transition just examined: by analyzing the necessary
reasons in actual revelation. His false start in
1 Dogmatics was to begin with man, with the possibility
of revelation, and so to show "reverence to false gods".
Now he will move from the necessary to the possible rather
than from the possible to the real. "It is not a matter
of things that must be said in advance, but of things
that must be said first" (I/1,41).[33] His quarrel with
even Reformed orthodoxy is that its dogmatics were "too
closely bound up with a form not taken from the thing
itself but from contemporary philosophies"; that is why
dogmatics must learn not from orthodoxy but from "Biblical
exegesis in the actual Reformers' school".[34]
What is Barth's paradigm case for this actuality of
revelation? It is the incarnate Word, the historical
appearance - not mere phenomenon (Erscheinung) but because of the special history surrounding and attesting
it (Heilsgeschichte), an unavoidable event (Ereignis).
This summary could be illustrated from innumerable sources
- notably the early chapters of Gifford Lectures, and especially the first volume of the K.D.[35] Because God is
a speaking Other, his self-revelation "has its reality and
truth wholly and in every respect - i.e. ontically and
noetically - within itself". (I/1,350). The biblical
testimony therefore constitutes "a self-contained novum",
with exegesis, as mentioned above, the way to begin theology. Barth is therefore committed to the most serious
grappling with the questions of time, history, and worldliness. He acknowledges here the help received from
Heinrich on these very issues;[36] but his massive and
consistent reflection is his own. Regin Prenter, comment-
ing on Bonhoeffer's charge of Offenbarungspositivismus,
seeks to honor that criticism by showing Barth's "actualism, analogism and universalism".[37] I believe there is
much weight to Prenter's analysis. Barth commits himself

to a theology of appearances, so to speak, according to
which revelation occurs in specific acts, not logically
connected in a series - what Prenter calls a "point by
point" view of revelation (je und je). If one does attempt a connection, a serial view, Barth calls it Religion - even Paul's Nomos is translated so.

Prenter's other terms, analogism and universalism,
refer to the "platonizing language which is also found
in the whole of the Church Dogmatics, in which there is
increasing reference to 'correspondence', analogy, like-
ness, image, etc." It is the supra-temporal nature of
revelation, according to this critique, which shows
Barth's transcendentalism, and therefore his choice of
cognition over being. Gustav Wingren has for long
levelled a similar charge against Barth, that he is preoccupied with epistemology, with a paradigm of Incarnation.
Although I would support this criticism to a degree, I
think Barth provides some excellent counter-arguments.
For one thing, he seems quite consistent in calling his
so-called analogism an "exegetical decision", taken
"under the compulsion of the object" of faith (II/1,227).
He points out that the error of "anthropomorphism" belongs not only to crude, bodily ideas of divinity, but
also to "spiritual" ideas - a point that Bonhoeffer himself makes in Creation and Fall. Moreover, his view of
revelation as demanding an appropriate order of reasoning - the "scientific" method - implies the necessity of
beginning with epistemology. Revelation gives, as "the
order intrinsic to the theme", not analysis of divine
being and then its activity ad extra, but the reverse:
the ordo cognoscendi first, followed by but still related
to, the ordo essendi (II/1,348ff). The passage is worth
quoting: "The logical rigour of the dialectic which occu-
pies us must not conceal from us the fact that we are not
concerned with any sort of dialectic but with the very
special dialectic of the revelation and being of God, in
the apprehension of which we are not left to chance or
caprice but must adjust ourselves to the order intrinsic
to the theme, or realised on it. It is important not to
miss this order if we are not to miss the thing itself".
Here is the Anselmic method indeed: the ultimate Truth
imposes its own ratio which guarantees the mind's conformity to its object only by the painstaking and painful
(a catharsis is inevitably involved) backtracking on the
way which this Truth has taken toward us. Analogy remains

43

"the correspondence of the unlike" (III/1,196). The
divine accommodation or condescension involves a gracious
opening of the Incomparable to certain analogies which
serve to mediate and to heal; but all are the result of
and therefore to be judged by, the mediator and healer,
Jesus Christ. "In the reality of this event (in der
Wirklichkeit dieses Ereignisses) God proves that He is
free to be our God" (I/2,1).

The final question, then, is Barth's paradigm case, as
philosophers would call it today, or the archetypal Ana-
logue, in classical terms. At this point I find Karl
Barth a most persuasive and attractive thinker. He knows
that he operates within a circle - even Tillich granted
that "kerygmatic theology" lies behind philosophical theology and describes the path to be followed. And if he
can show that he is a theologian because of the special
object to whose presence he witnesses, and because of the
special science to which it calls him, then he will have
made a prima facie case for his cavalier treatment of
philosophy. In short, he will have established the
autonomy of theology by identifying "God" in terms of a
paradigm case - a form of analogia analogans - namely,
Jesus Christ.(38) "Revelation does not differ from the
Person of Jesus Christ" (I/1,134); "Jesus is the Lord ...
can only be affirmed in an analytic proposition, as the
beginning of all thought about it" (I/1,465). The name
in question is a proper name, but it represents also the
divine freedom to name himself through the "worldliness"
which it involves. Here is the heart of any philosophical
critique of Barth, where he discusses language. For instance, in the sections in I/1 on this topic, Barth deals
with language in an "adoptionist" manner, as it were -
just as he will deal with "religion" in I/2 ("one religion
is adopted and distinguished as the true one before all
others", 339). The "worldliness" which characterizes all
the media of revelation means that the church is a socio-
logical entity, the Bible a document of history of religions, Rabbi Jesus a founder, while theology - listen! -
"so surely as it avails itself of human speech, is also
a philosophy or a conglomerate of all sorts of philosophy"
(I/1,188).

Does not Karl Barth want to have it both ways? He wishes
to be free from all taint of mere philosophy, and yet time
after time acknowledges the impossibility of that kind of
freedom. It were, he says, a "grotesque comedy" to accuse

44

others of this or that philosophy, for "It is no more
true of anyone that he does not mingle the Gospel with
some philosophy, than that here and now he is free from
all sin except through faith" (I/2,728). This section
(727ff) is a denial of every [sacrificium intellectus;]
that is, it is grace itself, Incarnation itself, which
implies a use of philosophy - otherwise sinful man would
cease from his sin, his worldliness, his situation in
time and space. Therefore, Barth concludes, everything
depends on "the How of this use" (730). And he makes it
clear that he wishes to leave the beginning of everything
up to scripture, to exegesis, so that in that light one
may judge philosophies, whether and when and how to use
them - and even Barth himself suggests, "I cannot radically exclude even the possibility that in certain circumstances, and for the better interpretation of Scripture, I myself will decide to use some quite different
hypothesis, and even have to become a more or less consistent 'convert' to a different philosophy" (731).

The trouble I have with Barth is that his crucial def-   — crit.
initions of both philosophy and science are too Kantian   Barth?
- that is, relative to and conditioned by this particular
philosophical option - to carry the absolutist freight
which Barth insists on. Philosophy, for him, is only a
limited and dialectical theory of knowledge; science is
that in which "an object is involved and a sphere of
activity".39

There are, however, alternative definitions for both
disciplines. Philosophy may, for instance, be dialectical
as in Hegel and Marx; it may also be logistical as in
Carnap or Russell; or inquiry as in James and Dewey.
Besides that threefold division, we should ponder process
philosophy's use of a Whiteheadian metaphysics, Maritain's
classical view of the "universal science of being", and
Husserl's Cartesian attempt to make philosophy "a strict
science". The aims of both Maritain and Husserl raise
the very question Barth is asking, perhaps unduly influenced by Scholz's concept of mathesis universalis
(or Leibniz, finally, with a scientia generalis): is not
theology the definitive science?40

Barth's loaded definitions of philosophy and science,
I maintain, pervert his otherwise attractive definition
of theology as the most beautiful science of all. His
"dogmatic science" depends on his Kantian epistemology

* To which the response is: is not this "How" then
either (a.) this how is non-rational (e.g. a kind of reliance on prayer)
or   (b.) it is rational, thus a method, thus a philosophy!
Thus the importance of clarifying dialectic.

45

-Re-
philos.

in which "views and concepts" (Anschauungen und Begriffe)
form the structure of human knowing. This structure is
given truth (Wahrhaftigheit) when it is "adopted and determined to participation in the truth of God by God
Himself in grace".[41] He bases this adoption on the principle that "God is known only through God" (Gott wird nur
durch Gott erkannt). But this principle - that religious
truth is self-evident - is not exclusively Christian, and
is as compatible with mysticism as with Christian orthodoxy.
Barth must face the harder question: is the Kantian epistemology the only adoptable one? If so, is this because
it is already baptized by Christian influences, i.e. a
crypto-biblical form of thought? That would be a subtle
form of theological imperialism, fraught with grave perils.
Or if not, then must not Barth admit that other structures
may prove adoptable, so that alternative dogmatics will
follow? It rather looks as if the Kantian philosophy
functions as natural theology for Barth; or to put it
another way, his criteria for adoptability are the "synthetic a priori" of his system, the hidden presupposition
of his definition of the theological enterprise.[42]

-Re-
Science

Barth's idea of science reflects another point in his
circular reasoning. He consistently defines dogmatics as
a science: "we find ourselves in basic opposition to
Philosophy, but we are all the closer methodologically to
the inductive sciences based on observation and inference".[43]
In his dogmatic prolegomena, however, he includes a section
on 'Dogmatics as a Science' (I/1.7) which protests against
restricting science to natural science. It would seem
that in general, Barth has in mind the German concept of
Wissenschaft - any consistent, disciplined intellectual
approach - rather than the narrower English concept of
science. But also, and in particular, Barth found science
in its more positive or natural or inductive variety more
compatible with his definition of theology as a special
case. T.F. Torrance's recent trilogy of writings on this
topic is most helpful here, not only because he has read
Barth's grand aim properly but also because he recognizes
the shift in "science" itself.[44] For, although Torrance
uses the word in the sense of a universal or "basic way
of knowing" which "applies to every area of human life
and thought",[45] he also appreciates the dramatic shift
in recent scientific method, in which induction has given
place to a renewed role for hypothetico-deductive models,

to what Michael Polanyi means by the "tacit dimension"
of knowledge, involved in the acceptance of "the logic
of discovery" (Karl Popper) as the new paradigm. But
if this is the form in which "science" appears today,
it looks much less adoptable as a complementary discipline
which knows its own limits, than Barth's image implies.
To speak of "dogmatic science" therefore is not to beg
a question so much as to tie oneself to a historical
curiosity.

CONCLUSIONS

I have held that first, Karl Barth (as well as Heinrich)
operates within a Kantian problématique, in that the polarity of real and idea, the dialectical structure of human
knowing, is accepted as the correct description; second,
the transitional work on philosophy and theology issued
in theological actualism, positing credal affirmations
as data for analytic thought; third, the aim of showing
the scientific nature of theology itself is part of a
Kantian package, and depends on tendentious definitions
of both philosophy and science (and theology).

A major conclusion of the above is that Barth's "dialogue" with philosophy is not just ambiguous but self-
deceiving. Thus on the one hand, he can study philosophers
with sympathy and insight - witness the beautiful portraits
of the first part of the Prot. Theologie im 19. Jahrhundert,
and the passages throughout Dogmatics III where he engages
Schopenhauer, Leibniz, Fichte, Nietzsche, Heidegger, Sartre.
On the other hand, he frustrates his dialogue by concluding - almost intoning - that their view, concerns, axioms
and goals have nothing in common with those of theology.
Even the "nothingness" of Heidegger and Sartre comes to
this: "seeing they do not really see" (III/3,348). Their
blindness seems to result from their refusing a theological beginning, for ultimately the Word of God operates
everywhere: philosophy "can be set in motion and then
have power to move" (I/2,735). Barth's own epistemology,
anthropology, ontology - and meontology! - constitute a
proper "seeing", on the other hand, because they are open
to a biblical starting-point.

A criterion of openness may appear pure, but in fact
it itself has a Kantian ring. It was Kant who ended the
classical tradition of philosophy as a way of obtaining
knowledge, substituting a critical philosophy which operates

47

up against the limiting concepts (freedom, immortality,
God for instance) that are reached by other means.[46]
Barth likewise employs the limiting concept (Grenzfall)
not only in his ethics[47] but in his theological analytic
itself. For "the knowledge which establishes Christian
language and doctrine" (II/1,186) involves a circularity
that is posited by a radical Transcendent, beyond all
limits and therefore in principle the absolute Noumenon.
As we have maintained, Barth is far from ignorant of his
situation. His dialectic of being and·act moves toward
a kind of "positivism of history" we might say, rather
than of "revelation" (although he answered Bonhoeffer:
"a little revelation-positivism is a good thing"). Where
he posits a ":third dimension" he breaks the Kantian dialectic, he moves around the epistemological circle far
enough to offer a better perspective. That would be a
matter for further exploration.
   Let the last word be more positive - and more cheerful.
In that same tribute to Heinrich, Karl stresses the co-
humanity (Mitmenschlichkeit) of philosopher and theologian.
Because neither can be "pure", both must work at common
or similar questions, characterized by humility, and by
humor. Each must resist the temptation to trade places
with the other, as crypto-theologian here and crypto-
philosopher there. In particular, when theologian plays
philosopher he surrenders his proper work of the science
of God: a crypto-philosopher, he states, is a pseudo-
theologian, contributing to a theological history which
becomes "a history of catastrophe". Barth's own zeal for
his beautiful science, his jealousy for the name of God,
his single-minded devotion to analysis of his paradigm-case,
have been salutary for us all. If we find cause to quarrel,
however deeply, let it be with similar humility and humor,
not unmindful that at this very moment a rejuvenated Karl
Barth is smiling at us - if he can take "time" to turn
away aside from listening to Mozart (in person!) "with
the angels".

NOTES

1   in G. Huber, ed., Philosophie und Christliche Exis-
     tenz: Festschrift für Heinrich Barth (Basel: Helbing
     and Lichtenhahn, 1960), pp. 93-106)

48

2   Ibid., 106
3   Foreword to Evangelical Theology: An Introduction
    (NY: Holt, Rinehart and Winston, 1963), p. xii
4   January 23, 1923; p.126 of Revolutionary Theology in
    the Making, ed. Jas. D. Smart (John Knox Press, 1964)
5   Henri Bouillard, Karl Barth, Vol. I, pp. 17ff (Aubier,
    1957); cf. T.F. Torrance, Karl Barth: An Introduction
    to his Early Theology, 1910-1931 (SCM, 1962), Part
    Two; and Karl Barth's speech Dank und Reverenz (E.T.
    Martin Rumscheidt, 'A Thank You and a Bow: Kierkegaard's
    Reveille' in The Canadian Journal of Theology, XI/1
    (1965)
6   The theologians treated in the second part of Die
    Prot. Theol. im 19 Jhdt. illustrate the anti-
    metaphysical tradition before Hermann, with which
    Karl Barth identified his work.
7   cf. Barth's Dortmund lectures, 1929, Schicksal und
    Idee in der Theologie (in Theologische Fragen und
    Antworten, E.V.Z. 1957); E. Brunner's Religions-
    philosophie evangelischer Theologie (E.T. The Phil-
    osophy of Religion, London 1937), esp. 59ff
8   Act and Being (London 1962 - Akt und Sein: Trans-
    zendentalphilosophie und Ontologie in der system-
    atischen Theologie, 1931), 83f
9   Philosophie der Praktischen Vernunft, 1927; Die
    Freiheit der Entscheidung im Denken Augustins, 1935;
    Philosophie der Erscheinung, 1946-and 1959 (complete
    Bibliography in Huber, op. cit., 251ff)
10 cf. on this whole problem Egon Brinkschmidt, Sören
    Kierkegaard und Karl Barth (Neukirchener Verlag,
    1970), esp. 67ff, 'Die Paradoxie'
11 'Dank und Reverenz', op. cit.
12 'Barth's Relation to Kierkegaard: Some Further Light',
    Canadian Journal of Theology (XIII/1,1967), p. 37
13 Revelation and Theology: An analysis of the Barth-
    Harnack Correspondence of 1923 (Cambridge U.P.,1972)
    esp. Part Two, Evaluation.
14 C.D. I/2, p. 322. Brunner's work (Tübingen, 1924)
    reduces Schleiermacher too much in the direction of
    the mystical, whereas Barth (e.g. Theology and Church,
    essay 'Schleiermacher', esp. 186ff) appreciates his
    commitment to the "cultural" pole. My point is that
    Barth had to wrestle with this polarity before he was
    able to develop the reflections in the C.D. I/2 (K.D.,
    1938). cf. also the essays in God, Grace and Gospel

about his transitional studies.

15 op. cit., pp. 133, 139
16 Schicksal und Idee, op. cit., section 1, pp. 62-72
17 Ibid., pp. 72-82
18 cf. H. Stahmer, Speak That I may See Thee (Macmillan, 1968)
19 pp. 82-92
20 Fides Quaerens Intellectum, Zürich 1931, I.4: Der Weg der Theologie (E.T., SCM, 1960)
21 op. cit., pp. 117,138f
22 Ibid., pp. 99, 116
23 At a "theologische Woche", Elberfeld, Heinrich lectured on October 8 and Karl on October 9, 1929. Heinrich's was 'Die Geistfrage im deutschen Idealismus'; Karl's, 'Zur Lehre vom Heiligen Geist'. The two addresses were published in a Beiheft of Zwischen den Zeiten (Beiheft 1, 1930). Karl's was translated by R. Birch Hoyle as The Holy Ghost and the Christian Life (London, 1938) which bibliographical references erroneously ascribe to both brothers.
24 Hoyle, op. cit., p. 59
25 Huber, op. cit., esp. 'Epochen', pp. 200-202
26 Ibid., 207
27 Philosophie der Erscheinung, Vol. I (Basel, 1947), p. 122; the context is a significant discussion of the Chórismos between Idee and Erscheinung in the Platonic tradition.
28 op. cit., esp. VI: Das Kontingente Sein
29 Vol. II, (Zweiter Teil: Neuzeit), pp. 433ff
30 loc. cit., pp. 242ff
31 cf. Ulrich Hedinger: Der Freiheitsbegriff in der K.D. Karl Barths (Zürich, 1962), pp. 172ff for the remarkable accord of the two brothers on this point.
32 How I Changed My Mind (John Knox Press, 1966) p. 62: speaking of his two theologian-sons, "The sun now constantly finds at least one of our family awake and at work in the service of the most beautiful of all sciences".
33 References in parentheses will be to volumes and pages of the Church Dogmatics in E.T.
34 Foreword to Heinrich Heppe's Reformed Dogmatics (E.T., London, 1950), p. vi.
35 The Knowledge of God and the Service of God (London, 1938), esp. II: The One God; Church Dogmatics I/1, 28ff on the starting point for dogmatics; 226ff on 'The

Word of God and Experience'; II/2, sect. 13, on Christ
as 'Objective Reality' and 'Objective Possibility'
(in that order) of revelation

36 C.D. I/2, pp. 45ff

37 'Dietrich Bonhoeffer and Karl Barth's Positivism of
Revelation' transl. by Martin Rumscheidt, in World
Come of Age, ed. R.G. Smith (London, 1967). cf. Martin
Storch on this question, chapter 1 of his Exegesen und
Meditationen zu Karl Barths K.D. (München, 1964)

38 One of my doctoral students helped clarify this point
- David Lochhead, The Autonomy of Theology, unpublished
McGill University Ph.D. thesis, 1966, chapter 4, 'The
Identification of God' (p. 44 above)

39 Dogmatics in Outline, p. 9

40 cf. Torrance, Theological Science, 107ff, 'General and
Special Sciences' and the final chapter, 'Theological
Sciences among the Special Sciences'

41 C.D. II/1, section 27, 'The Limits of our Knowledge
of God'

42 At the Colloquium, David Lochhead and Herbert Richardson
wished me to press this charge, of Barth's alleged
"synthetic apriori". I prefer to remain more cautious
on this point, since Barth's reading of Anselm itself
faces the issue, as well as his self-consciousness
about prolegomena. But I agree that the logic of my
criticism is to show that Barth is essentially Kantian
in bringing to the theological enterprise a theory of
knowledge which functions as the apriori, the categories, in his theology

43 C.D. III/2, p. 12. In this brief excursus Barth gives
a clear definition of science: "Exact science dedicated
to its object and its method, working positively and
not dreaming and romancing, is in fact pure knowledge
...". Now this itself is a form of positivistic philosophy of science, especially suited to natural science.
Where science pushes on, e.g. to claim that a physio-
logical description of brain is a contribution to
normative studies of mind, how would Barth's criteria
operate?

44 T.F. Torrance, Theological Science; Space, Time and
Incarnation; God and Rationality

45 God and Rationality, p. 91

46 cf. Barth's essay on Kant in Die Prot. Theol. im 19.
Jhdt. It is strange that Barth wishes there had been
someone with "insight, courage and humour" to remind

*. Throw out the essay I have experienced this "caution" as a
certain lack of resolution or clarity.

51

Kant that the "irony" of placing philosophy and theology side by side has implications for both subjects; for J.G. Hamann (who, with Kierkegaard, is ignored in this book) did this very thing to his friend Kant.

47 cf. John Yoder, <u>Karl Barth and the Problem of War</u> (Abingdon, 1970) for a critical evaluation of Barth's reliance on the <u>Grenzfall</u> as paradigm

PAUL L. LEHMANN

The Concreteness of Theology: Reflections on the
Conversation Between Barth and Bonhoeffer

There is an amusing story about the last earthly meeting
between Karl Barth and Paul Tillich. The story may be
entirely apocryphal. Nevertheless, it seems pertinent
to our present assignment, and hence, a guarded currency
may be accorded it. It seems that after a cordial and
mellow visit to Barth in the Bruderholzweg, Barth accompanied Tillich to the nearby Haltestelle of the
Basler Strassenbahn. As they walked along together,
Barth put his arm around Tillich's shoulder and remarked:
"Paulus, as I think about our conversation, it occurs to
me that perhaps the real difference between your theology
and mine could be explained with reference to the legend
inscribed above the portico of the Church of the Nativity
in Jerusalem. Hic verbum caro factum est! Now, Paulus",
Barth went on, "you see, I have to have my hic!"
   Whatever may be the case with respect to Paul Tillich,
this "hic!" is certainly at issue -- perhaps decisively
at issue - between Karl Barth and Dietrich Bonhoeffer.
More critically still, this "hic!" is decisively at issue
in the doing of theology today. Abrasive as that phrase
is, to ears and sense accustomed to the ennobling ca-
dences of the Queen's English, it does express the perceptive and subtle evangelical sensibility of the author
of the Fourth Gospel. "But he who does what is true",
says the third chapter, at verse 21, "comes to the light,
that it may be clearly seen that his deeds have been
wrought in God." Or, as the New English Bible puts it:
"the honest man comes to the light so that it may be
clearly seen that God is in all he does." The integrity,
indeed, the possibility of theology today hang upon that
"seeing clearly"; upon seeing in and with the clarity of
light, as against the shadowy vagueness or the obscurity
of darkness, -- seing -- not God -- but what God is doing
in the world; and so, who God is. According to the
Fourth Gospel, the who of God is clearly seen in the.
doing of God who "so loved the world that he gave his
only Son, that whoever believes in him should not perish
but have eternal life." (3:16)[1] Barth's own way of
trying to take dogmatic account of this doing and seeing,

53

and explicitly of this text is to say that "God is He
who freely loves".[2] As if to underscore the "hic!"
which he has to have, Barth underlines the Vulgate rendering of the outos gar with which 3:16 begins. Sic!
enim, says the Vulgate. Barth's "hic!" is this "sic"![3]
   In a different context, namely not the writing of
Dogmatics but the struggle of a church in statu confessionis
with the principalities and powers in the heavenly and
earthly places of this world, Bonhoeffer makes the same
point. Speaking of "rigoristic and idealistic" misinter-
pretations of the Bible, Bonhoeffer asked in 1942: "But
how is it, then, with John 3:16? ... The genuine relation between congregation (Gemeinde) and world develops
only in faith in the revelation of God in the world."[4]
Four years earlier, the point had been made with reference to 3:21. "The Bible", Bonhoeffer declared, "knows
nothing at all about the pathos and problematic of the
question concerning 'our way'. Our way ... has no weight
of its own, no problematic of its own, and in particular
no tragedy (Tragik) of its own. It is simply 'doing the
truth' (John 3:21), wherein the accent falls wholly on
the side of the truth. ... Along this way, to let Jesus
Christ find us, this is our way."[5]
   Whether one identifies the "truth" in the doing of
theology with reference to "the Bible", or to "the revelation of God in the world", or to the "Who-ness" of the
"God who freely loves", or to the "deeds which have been
wrought in God", -- the hic! seems somehow insistently
to haunt us. Try as it will, theology seems unable to
get the hic! and the sic! together without succumbing
either to the flamboyancy of rhetoric or to the tedium
of repetition. As Thomas Mendip in Mr. Christopher Fry's
"The Lady is Not For Burning" stridently declaims: "O
tedium, tedium, tedium ... Where in this small-talking
world can I find a longitude with no platitude?"[6] Somehow since Bultmann and Wittgenstein, and Norbert Wiener
and Marshall McLuhan, and especially since Paul Ricoeur
and Ernst Bloch have cut a door into Huit Clos! and
lighted some alternatives to existentialism, we have begun to learn to live with ambiguities and semantic subtle-
ties, with symbolizations and even paradoxes. But what
disquiets us to the point of embarrassment and accelerates
the flight from church and parish, from theology and
prayer is the tantalizingly elusive concreteness without
which no hic! commands its sic!; and every sic! -- as in

the whispering gallery of London's old St. Paul's --
echoes with intensifying faintness the echoless hic! to
which it once belonged.

Perhaps the nadir of our declining sensibility of the
concreteness indispensable to the significance and integrity of theology arrived in the course of a discussion
in my own theological faculty in late May of the present
year. Engaged as we had been, during the months preceding, with a concentrated and determined re-ordering of
our theological, educational and institutional priorities
for the immediate and for the long-range future, it was
inevitable and understandable that the question of a new
design for the program of studies and involvements leading to the Master of Divinity degree should be high on
the agenda. Without waiting for the agenda to elicit a
nihil obstat!, an ad hoc group of faculty and students
undertook to explore "the perimeters and the parameters,
the feasibilities and the negotiabilities", as the current
idiom vocalizes where we are and where we want to go. At
year-end in May, the faculty at large was invited to share
in a conversation about these idiomatic projections. Some
of us responded; and we learned that the focus was to be
on the "American experience" for the basic reason that
this is where we all were, and where we all came in, when
the doing of theology was what we were to be about. At
one point in the conversation, a black colleague expressed
some reservations about this point of entry into theological inquiry and explained that the "American experience"
effectively excluded his people who for three hundred
years in the United States had been effectively excluded
from the "American experience". Why, he then went on to
ask, had the ad hoc group not considered the Bible? The
Bible, he went on to explain, was where his people were,
and where they all came in, when the doing of theology was
what they were to be about. A long silence followed;
after which, two colleagues very much at the center of the
re-ordering of our priorities, replied by saying that they
would like to begin with the Bible but for them the Bible
was simply too remote to be of formative significance for
their own theological work. "But how is it, then, with
John 3:16?" What about the "Who-ness" of the "God who
freely loves"? or about coming "to the light, that it may
be clearly seen that (one's) deeds have been wrought in
God"? Clearly, where I live and work, the sic! is on a
runaway course in search of an authenticating hic!, with

expectations at once eager and hesitant, frenetic and
wistful, political and pluralistic. And this search
goes on with a sobering candor matched by a sobering dis-
proportion between theological self-confidence and theological seriousness! It's all as though Karl Barth and
Dietrich Bonhoeffer had never lived and worked and died
at all! Or is it because, precisely because, of what they
did and did not do that our theological existence today
is devoid of persuasive and freeing concreteness and vulnerable to idolatrous and cultic concretenesses filling
the vacuum in our theological discrimination? It is as
if "the unclean spirit has gone out of" us, and finding
no rest, returns to find the house "empty, swept, and put
in order. Then he goes and brings with him seven other
spirits more evil than himself, and they enter and dwell
there; and the last state of that man shall be worse than
the first." Matthew, then, adds what Luke omits: "So
shall it be also with this evil generation."7

Let us, then, attempt to "make the best use of (our)
time" allotted to us by this gladdening occasion, "despite all the difficulties of these days". (Ephesians
5:16. Phillips) In doing so, let us attend in turn; (1)
to the question of concreteness in theology; (2) to the
relations between Barth and Bonhoeffer, as they were affected by this question; and (3) to some indication of a
way ahead as regards the concreteness of theology, setting
out, as we must, from where we are.

(1) THE QUESTION OF CONCRETENESS IN THEOLOGY

Although Barth and Bonhoeffer may have failed us as regards the question of concreteness in theology; and how-
soever one may interpret the point at issue between them
in their own debate, it can scarcely be denied that the
concreteness of theology was a major concern of their
theological work. In this concern, Barth and Bonhoeffer
are still very contemporary; and whatever alternatives may
now emerge (and some are emerging) can scarcely be serious
alternatives in disregard of Karl Barth and Dietrich
Bonhoeffer. Unable to re-read the Kirchliche Dogmatik from
beginning to end for this occasion, and also unable to
apply a computorial count to its pages, I have had to content myself with a scanning of the same. The survey shows
that in the Prolegomena, the words: konkret, Konkretheit,
together with their Latin equivalents: in concreto,

concretissimum, concretissime, occur with conspicuous
frequency. One encounters these terms with somewhat less
frequency but no less noticeably as far as III/4. Less
frequently and less noticeably, the words occur throughout volume four. If, then, one takes into account,
konkret, Konkretheit, in concreto, concretissimum, concretissime and their cognates, e.g. Gegenstaendlichkeit,
Wirklichkeit, Aktualitaet, Besonderheit, and the very
frequent "nicht in abstracto", it is not too much to say
that the driving pre-occupation of the Kirchliche Dogmatik is with the question of concreteness in theology.[8]
That this is the case, is obliquely attested by the
Registerband of the Kirchliche Dogmatik, which contains
no entry marked: Konkretheit or concretum. Otherwise,
the omission would be regrettable in itself, and also as
an oblique indication of a subliminal disregard, on the
part of the editors of the Registerband, of a widening
distance between the Kirchliche Dogmatik and that "something major in the wind that is 'hammering our lives and
psyches into new and unfamiliar shapes'."[9] In the writings
of Bonhoeffer, as is well known, the question of concreteness is the focal point of his Ethics, for which his two
major earlier books, Sanctorum Communio (1930) and Akt und
Sein (1931) prepare the way, and from which the Widerstand
und Ergebung (1951) delineates a movement towards involvement in a genuine worldliness.[10]
   Yet two recent assessments of our present theological
situation explicitly assert that the passion for concreteness which marked the theological work of Barth and
Bonhoeffer has been spent or misspent. It is not clear
which; but the consequences are the same. An article in
the April issue of Theology Today asserts "the powerlessness of the western intellectual tradition, as it is now
appropriated by us, to integrate and make sense of people's
experience, to mobilize us for the tasks we face. The
prophetic-apostolic witness, as part of this tradition,
shares in its powerlessness ... Barth's theology," the
article continues, "conceived originally only as a
prolegomenon, became a massive system, and the old categories of thought, which arose to interpret human experience in earlier times, were reinstated. ... This road
is closed to us."[11] The intellectual shift in our present
cultural situation, which the authors of the piece in
Theology Today underline, has been companioned by a socio-
political shift in our cultural situation stressed in the

course of the published meditations on the Fourth Gospel
by Professor Frederick Herzog of Duke University, which
arrived as this essay was in preparation. It is not
merely co-incidental that neither Karl Barth nor Dietrich
Bonhoeffer appear in the Index to Herzog's book. "The
debate on revelation in twentieth century Protestant
Theology", Herzog observes, "has been confounded by the
fact that revelation was understood as disclosure of something that is hidden not only in fact, but also in principle. As we have seen, however, God is not hidden in
principle. ... It is man's sin that hides God. The
presence and future of God always reach man. The real
trouble is that man does not acknowledge it."[12] Herzog's
call is for "a re-ordering of theological priorities";
and this in serious and unfailing recognition of the fact
that "In this society one cannot be a decent human being
(Ernst Bloch). In this church one cannot be a decent
christian . ... Theology today must begin with the wretched
of the earth, the marginales, the marginal figures of life
who are still struggling for personhood and dignity."[13]
To begin here means, for us in the United States, as
Herzog sees it, that "it is in the dialectical tension
between black and white theology and in their confrontation that today we must take up again the task to describe
what theology is all about."[14] Like the authors of the
article in Theology Today, Professor Herzog wants and
seeks to "narrow the gap between man's experience of faith
and man's experience in history".[15] But unlike the authors
of the article, Herzog thinks that there is an opening in
the road, an opening provided at least, by the Fourth
Gospel's version of the prophetic-apostolic witness. "...
In the Fourth Gospel", he says, "we can almost touch with
our hands the first full-fledged theological wrestling
with Jesus of Nazareth as liberator. The pristine movement of Christian thought becomes important for us, so
that our theological thinking might become more primal
too."[16]
   Clearly, these assessments of our present theological
situation are preoccupied, as were Barth and Bonhoeffer,
with the question of concreteness in theology. It is, in
our view, regrettable that they have found it necessary to
set the work of Barth and Bonhoeffer aside, however moment-
arily. Yet the theological seriousness, with which this
disregard has been accepted as necessary, calls for a re-
ciprocal theological seriousness towards the concerns about

concreteness, which inform these assessments. To set
these concerns aside with insensitive disregard, would
mean a failure to discern the sense in which Barth and
Bonhoeffer have not been overtaken by events in their
own wrestling with the question of concreteness in
theology. If such discernment were to be granted us, we
should then also be able in some measure to point the
way toward serious alternatives in distinction from alternatives insufficiently attentive to what Barth and
Bonhoeffer have committed to us.

What, then, is the question of concreteness in theology
all about? Among the remarkable qualities of the recently
published Random House unabridged Dictionary is the vivid-
ness, directness and conciseness with which it exposes
the semantic core of its entries. Thus, concreteness is
defined as "constituting an actual thing or instance; real,
pertaining to or concerned with realities or actual instances rather than abstractions."[17] With regard to instances or realities, to names as a class, in distinction
from the qualities pertaining to them, the class is said
to be concrete, the quality is said to be abstract. The
word, man, for example, is concrete; the word, human, is
abstract. It may be that no more is going on here than
the differentiation between nouns and adjectives. But
even if we suppose this to be the case, the distance between some adjectives and their nouns is greater than in
the case of others. A more conspicuous abstraction occurs.
The adjective "human", for instance, is less abstract
when applied to the noun man than is the adjective, intelligent. Witness the lively debate now going on between Jean Piaget and Jerome Brunner over the what and
the how of learning; or the intriguingly esoteric debate
over the relation between syntax and reality which seems
increasingly to be dividing Noam Chomsky from his students,
and the brightest ones at that![18] The pertinence of these
syntactical and pedagogical disputes over actualities or
realities, i.e., over concreteness, to the question of concreteness in theology is the companionship which they offer
theology in the misery of responsible analysis and interpretation; in what the Roemerbrief calls: die Krisis der
Erkenntnis" (under the rubric of "die Schuld der Kirche")
and die Krisis des freien Lebensversuchs (under the rubric
of "die grosse Stoerung"); in what Bonhoeffer's Ethik calls:
Gestaltung and die Struktur des vertantwortlichen Lebens.[19]
More importantly, however, this reminder of the rabies

scholarum humanorum to which the semantics of concreteness
point, should underline the possibility that God just
could be in somewhat better case. The theological tradition, however one may verbalize it, has insisted, at
least since Paul of Tarsus, that God is the center and
sum of all actuality and possibility, i.e., the "class"
who is the beginning and the end of all "classification";
sic! concreteness. God's omniscience embraces both his
fore-knowledge and his fore-ordination, so that both as
primus agens and as summum bonum, he is concretissimus
supremus sive absolutus. This can, of course, be a very
abstract way of thinking and speaking, even concretissime.
But let those who hasten too quickly to judge it as a
terminal case of hic-amnesia pause to consider the possible impoverishment of their own capacity to discern
the difference between the sound of words and their referentiality; as well as their own loss of cultural memory.
Nevertheless, where theology falters in its task is not
at the point of the concreteness of its warrant but in a
fluctuating openness and steadfastness towards the concretissimus (be he object?, subject?, revelatus?, ab-
sconditus?: in fact? or in principle?) who is Alpha and
Omega and Immanuel: behind and before and in the midst.

Thus, our colleagues, who through the pages of Theology
Today have rightly been pressing hard the question of
concreteness in theology "from somewhere along the road",
might find it possible to discern, precisely in their
situation as homines viatores, that intersection of two
worlds in Jesus Christ, from which the Roemerbrief sets
out,[20] and in the light of which, the KD is not really a
massive system designed to enthrone old categories but a
conversation of the people of God in all times and places
about the God who takes time to be with people on journey
and so meets them on the road. Surely this conversation
in other times and places must be allowed to call us into
question in our time and place as readily as we are called
to call that conversation into question from where we are
on the road. Just so, it may be that it has been given
to these colleagues, exactly along their road, to rejoice
in their deliverance from "programmatic" and "speculative"
abstractions; and in their calling, to risk "the bold endeavor to speak about the way in which the form of Jesus
Christ takes form in our world ... Concrete judgments
and decisions will have to be ventured here. Decision
and action can here no longer be delegated to the personal

conscience of the individual. Here there are concrete
commandments and instructions for which obedience is de-
manded."[21] Perhaps also, Professor Herzog, with like bold-
ness, might find in his "political theology", which seeks
to begin with "the wretched of the earth", neither an alternative to nor a displacement of "the great negative"
and "the great positive possibility", with which der
Roemerbrief concludes.[22] Perhaps in the very midst of
the tension between those possibilities, a tertium quid
may be discerned beyond God's hiddenness "in principle"
or "in fact". The mystery of presence and pressure upon
"the world of time and space and things, our world"[23], -
under which and by which the marginales are being liberated,
and to be liberated, for the human-ness which is their
righteousness and their destiny, - transcends, in its
sovereign majesty and purpose (its incomprehensibile and
its incognito), the unrighteousness and suffering and sin
in our world, and condescends in the miracle of Christmas,
to be involved in that world, concretissime: vere deus,
vere homo.[24] That happening -- then, and now -- is the
center and occasion of a Magnificat -- again concretissime
-- both in song and in the basic sense and structure of
things. "The structure of responsible life", wrote
Bonhoeffer, "is conditioned by two factors; life is bound
to man and to God and a man's own life is free... Jesus
Christ is man and is God in one. In him there takes place
the original and essential encounter with man and with
God. Henceforward man cannot be conceived and known otherwise than in the human form of Jesus Christ. In Him we see
humanity as that which God has accepted, borne and loved,
and as that which is reconciled with God. In Him we see
God in the form of the poorest of our brothers. There is
no 'man in himself,' just as there is no God 'in Himself';
both of these are empty abstractions. Man is the man who
was accepted in the incarnation of Christ, who was loved,
condemned and reconciled in Christ; and God is God become
man. There is no relation to men without a relation to
God and no relation to God without a relation to men, and
it is only our relation to Jesus Christ which provides
the basis for our relation to men and to God. Jesus Christ
is our life, and so now, from the standpoint of Jesus
Christ, we say that our fellow-man is our life and that
God is our life."[25] Surely, it will have escaped no one
that this is virtually a verbatim re-statement of the
apostolic summation which Paul of Tarsus sent along to

the congregation at Corinth: "With us, therefore, worldly
standards have ceased to count in our estimate of any man;
even if once they counted in our understanding of Christ,
they do so now no longer. When anyone is united to Christ,
there is a new world; the old order has gone, and a new
order has already begun."[26] Thus, from a pauline, as well
as from a johannine perspective, "concrete judgments and
decisions will have to be ventured here". If, and in so
far as, theology today must begin with the wretched of
the earth, it is because "a new order has already begun".
To begin here in theology is precisely to risk "the bold
endeavor to speak about the way in which Jesus Christ
takes form in our world". There are companions in this
endeavor of whom Professor Herzog need not take account
but who are not, on that account, less companions in the
same theological venture concretely to make Jesus Christ
concrete.

The distance between Barth and Bonhoeffer and their
successors in the generation following is not marked by
the presence or absence of a concern for the question of
concreteness in theology. Where Jesus Christ is the concrete focus of the concreteness of theology, there need
be no "middle wall of partition", (Eph. 2:14. AV). Instead, what Barth and Bonhoeffer have done, and what their
successors are strongly urging must be done differently,
is exactly what the concreteness of theology is all about.
The profound disquiet over the abstractness of theology,
which erupted in the Reformation, and then took a wrong
turn from which the theologians of the nineteenth century
had to rescue it, has come significantly into view with
Barth and Bonhoeffer. It is the insistence by Barth and
Bonhoeffer, upon the "actual instance" and "the realities
pertaining to it" (Random House) that has brought the
question of concreteness in theology to the present critical juncture. This juncture could be described in the
following way: Barth and Bonhoeffer are being asked by
the oncoming theologians in our time to make sense of
Jesus Christ in the midst of the culture and experience
of a "world come of age"; whereas Barth and Bonhoeffer,
in their turn, are asking the oncoming theologians in our
time to make sense of the culture and experience of a
"world come of age" with due regard to the concrete presence
and pressure of Jesus Christ in our midst, "the same yesterday, today, and forever" (Heb. 13:8). If Barth and
Bonhoeffer seem at a critical distance to have been unable

to bring their clearly resounding hic!, and a no less
clearly resounding sic!, persuasively together, the task
before their wistful and/or impatient critics is to match,
with no less persuasiveness, their understandable passion
for an unmistakeable sic!, with a corresponding passion
for an irresistible, albeit dialectical, hic!

(2) THE RELATIONS BETWEEN BARTH AND BONHOEFFER

At this critical juncture, the relations between Barth
and Bonhoeffer on the question of concreteness in theology
may be looked at afresh. We need not review the story of
these relations beyond the reminder of Eberhard Bethge's
succinct account of their stages.[27] Bethge's account makes
it plain that the principal concern which informed both
their theological kinship and their theological disquiet
towards one another, was the concern for the concreteness
of revelation.[28]

Barth's first explicit reference to their kinship in
this concern noted with approval Bonhoeffer's interpretation of the imago dei in Creation and Fall. There, the
concreteness of the Creator's relation to his special
creature is evident in the relation between male and female -- in the discreteness of each and in their reci-
procity.[29] The special ethics takes account of Bonhoeffer's
ethics as a genuine advance in exploring the concrete relations between the vertical and the horizontal factors in
Christian faith and action. "Only insofar as the vertical
intersects a horizontal can there be a genuine vertical",
Barth wrote. "Due attention must be given to this horizontal, and on that account also to the specificity
(Stetigkeit) and continuity of the divine command as well
as of human action."[30] Bonhoeffer's notion of the mandates
seemed to Barth to do just that and to illuminate, for
example, Bonhoeffer's penetrating psychological and human
interpretation of suicide, as well as to explain his participation in political assassination.[31] Barth's highest
praise for Bonhoeffer appears in the penultimate volume
of the Kirchliche Dogmatik, in the course of his own account of the communio sanctorum. Here, the Nachfolge,
and even more, despite its sharp criticism of Barth, the
Sanctorum Communio are impressively applauded, and with an
open-ness which is not diminished by lingering reservations.[32] With reference to what Bonhoeffer called
"einfaeltiger Gehorsam" (single-minded obedience), Barth

declares: "That obedience is single-minded, in which a
man simply does what is commanded: no more and no less,
and nothing other than just that."[33] Barth agrees with
Bonhoeffer that this is the concreteness of radical
obedience.

From Bonhoeffer's side, the kinship with Barth started
with the Roemerbrief. As Bonhoeffer began his teaching
in Berlin in the winter semester of the year 1931/32, he
addressed himself to the "History of systematic Theology
in the 20th Century". The concluding section was devoted
to the question "Where do we stand today?" "In the whole
of the more recent literature", he remarked, "Barth has
not been taken with sufficient seriousness. ... Perhaps
in the Roemerbrief, the peril of proximity to neo-Kantian
transcendentalism was not always clearly seen by Barth.
But he begins with the concrete revelation; and where
Natorp and Tillich say, 'No God' (Nicht-Gott), Barth must
say, 'Jesus Christ'."[34] The significance of this remark
is that it comes at the beginning of Bonhoeffer's own
career as a theological teacher and within six months
after the sharp attacks upon Barth in Akt und Sein, and
a year and a half after searching questions put to Barth
in Sanctorum Communio. Five years later, an exchange of
letters, initiated by Bonhoeffer and replied to by Barth
conveys in a lively way Bonhoeffer's concern for the actuality of doing theology with full candor towards the
increasingly troublesome distance between theological
students and the scriptural and dogmatic tradition. In
turn, Barth replied with an openness and flexibility in
the doing of theology which greatly impressed his younger
colleague and critic. "The questions", wrote Bonhoeffer,
"which young theologians seriously raise today are: how
do I learn to pray? how do I learn to read the Bible?
Either we can help them at these points or we cannot help
them at all. ... Of course, these matters presuppose at
the same time real and serious and unadulterated theological, exegetical and dogmatic work. I am clear about
that. ... But I do not wish to by-pass these questions
(ueberhoeren) for anything in the world..." To this,
Barth replied: "Surely you will not expect from me anything
but openness toward the substance of theology (Sache) and
at the same time that I view it with concern. I am open
because it is clear to me that in doctrine and in life always new questions must be asked, new attempts must be
made... My concern arises from the experience of the past

fifteen years which has found me under the steady fire of
objections, and 'concerns', and amplifications ... the
fundamental correctness of which I never could deny or
wish to deny, but in the concrete explication of which
... I have become more critical because I have seen more
clearly that ... such better solutions are like losing
the sparrow in hand for the sake of the pigeon on the
roof." What impressed Bonhoeffer was "how this man was
able 'when necessary (noetigenfalls) to correct his
notebooks."[35]

So Barth and Bonhoeffer seem to circle towards and then
around each other out of their common and kindred concern
for the question of concreteness in theology. For both,
the concreteness of theology is its calling to make plain
in and for the community of believers, which is the church,
and in and for the world, the reality of God disclosed in
his human-ness in Jesus Christ. Barth worries about
Bonhoeffer's exploration and description of this concreteness, owing to what Barth regards as insufficient safeguards against the loss of the specificity of Jesus Christ.
Bonhoeffer, on the other hand, worries about Barth's exploration and description of this concreteness, owing to
what Bonhoeffer regards as insufficient safeguards against
the loss of the human specifics to which the specificity
of Jesus Christ is directed and with which it is involved.
"Barth was never really comfortable with Bonhoeffer's
directness"; writes Bethge, "he much preferred eschatological limits (Begrenztheit durch die Eschata)."[36] According to Bethge, this may very well have been the point at
issue, succinctly stated, about which Bonhoeffer wrote to
Erwin Sutz, after his meeting with Barth in Berlin in
April 1932. "Barth, however," he wrote, "does not agree
with me on this point. This is now clear to me. Nevertheless, he raised the point again with me recently, and
asked whether I still thought along this line. And he
made it plain enough that for him, this point was still
uncomfortable."[37] Uncomfortable though it was, as late as
1936, in the letter to which we have already referred,
Barth could say: "And now I see already that another wave
is gathering, especially among the youth of the Confessing
Church (Bekenntniskirche), in which then everything that
has gone before will acquire new actuality, and it could
even be that you are probably called and equipped to be
spokesman and leader. If it should turn out this time to
be no empty noise (blinder Laerm), I would hope not yet to

65

be too old this time to learn what has to be learned, and
necessarily to correct my notebooks, as I have already
done in other respects. Meanwhile, however, you must
understand if I simply wait."[38]

In this context, the increasing tension between Barth
and Bonhoeffer over the question of concreteness must be
understood. There is, we suggest, a link between the
issue sharply raised in Akt und Sein and the hasty remark
from the cell at Tegel, which greatly irritated Barth,
and which those whom slogans fascinate, prefer to remember rather than to understand. In Akt und Sein, the
passionate Lutheran engaged the unyielding Calvinist over
the finitum capax sive incapax infiniti. From Tegel came,
on the 30 April 1944, the vigorous letter to Bethge, in
the course of which Bonhoeffer declared with regard to
the relations between religion and Christianity, for
which he was himself on the way to the phrase "religionless Christianity", that "Barth, who alone had begun to
think along these lines, after all did not think these
ideas through or carry them out, but arrived instead at
a positivism of revelation, which in the last analysis,
remained after all, a restoration (Restauration)." A week
later came a more passionate, not to say intemperate,
outburst on the same matter. "Barth", said Bonhoeffer,
"was the first theologian -- and this remains his great
achievement -- to begin the criticism of religion. But
then, in its place, he set up a positivistic doctrine of
revelation according to which the mandate is: 'eat, bird,
or die' (friss, Vogel, oder stirb). Whether the doctrine
concerns the Virgin Birth or the Trinity, or whatever,
each doctrine is an equal and necessary part of the whole,
that must, then, be swallowed as a whole or not at all.
This is not biblical."[39]

The crucial point at stake in the tension over the
finitum capax sive incapax infiniti is this: if the majesty
and freedom of God towards the creation are too consistently stressed, the reality of faith on the part of God's
human creature tends to be too radically called into
question. The consequence is that the concrete humanness
of Jesus Christ as God's concrete way of being God for us
is obscured. On the other hand, if the reality of faith,
as the direct experience of God in his concrete humanness
towards man is too consistently stressed, the freedom and
majesty of God, in the radicality of their priority and
initiative tend to be insufficiently attended to. In the

latter instance, the mystery of God's concreteness in his
self-revelation loses theological force. "... the desire
to locate in the act of belief itself the reflection which
discovers faith only in the reflected form of faith-wishfulness, that is the danger of Barth. Faith and 'faith-
wishfulness' lie together in the same act. Every act of
faith is 'wishful' in so far as it is a happening embedded
in the psychic and there accessible to reflexion. But
faith properly so-called lies in the act's intention towards Christ, which is founded in being in the communion
of Christ. A faith which grows doubtful of itself because it considers itself unworthy is a faith which stands
in temptation. ... All praying, all searching for God in
his Word, all clinging to his promise ..., all hoping in
sight of the Cross, all this for reflexion is 'religion',
'faith-wishfulness'; but in the communion of Christ, while
it is still the work of man, it is God-given faith, faith
willed by God, wherein by God's mercy he may really be
found. If faith wished to question its own sufficiency
it would already have lapsed from intentionality into
temptation."[40] This very Lutheran account of what we
have since learned to call the existential reality of
faith is what Bonhoeffer meant by his insistence upon
the finitum capax infiniti. When Barth insisted upon the
finitum incapax infiniti, he was exploring primarily the
knowledge of God -- in faith and through faith, to be
sure -- but as a cognitive act. For him, the neglect of
the incapax on this front was tantamount to a natural
theology which compromised the majesty and freedom of God
in his self-revelation in Jesus Christ. For Barth, the
incapax protected the concreteness of God in his revelation, as it were, on the giving end of the stick. For
Bonhoeffer, the capax protected the concreteness of the
revelation of God, as it were, on the receiving end of
the stick, that is, in the reality of faith. For both,
the major question of theology was the question of concreteness.

The failure of Barth and Bonhoeffer to meet on this
issue underlies their more intense misunderstanding on
the matter of revelational positivism. The gap had
widened because of Bonhoeffer's increasing pre-occupation
with the bond between concreteness and non-religiousness.
The question: how can one speak in a non-religious way
about God? about Jesus Christ? breathes through every
line of the intense letter to Bethge. Somehow the reality

of the communion of saints had come to include for
Bonhoeffer both believers and unbelievers because God
was and could be experienced in his concreteness in humiliation rather than in majesty, in suffering rather than
in sovereignty, at the center rather than on the edges
of life. This was the Lutheran view of faith as a lively
trust in the miracle of Christmas and of Crucifixion trans-
posed to the context of a world come of age. For
Bonhoeffer, it is the reality of faith, however real its
knowledge may be, which excludes every kind of positivism
in theology. It is not surprising that Bonhoeffer should
have missed this kind of concreteness in the KD, especially
in the Prolegomena. Barth's own specific attention to
these concerns did not emerge until III/2 (1949) and in
III/4 (1951) and IV/2 (1959), where also his positive appraisal of Bonhoeffer occurs. By then, it was too late
for further exchange on these matters. It remains surprising, however, that Bonhoeffer should have read and
heard in and through Barth's epistemological pre-occupa-
tions mainly and strongly their positivistic leanings and
implications. This is surprising, not least because of
Bonhoeffer's expressed satisfaction with Barth's Anselm
Book;[41] but most of all because of their common involvement in the struggle of the Confessing Church against the
idolatry and tyranny of National Socialism. Without the
Barmen Declaration, there would scarcely have been a pro-
tracted, life and death church struggle; and without the
KD, there would scarcely have been Barmen. The record
suggests that the KD, far from being or functioning as a
massive positivist imposition to be swallowed whole, and
all or nothing, was in fact a theological arsenal for political conflict and liberation which made possible concretissime a confrontation between God concretely revealed
in Jesus Christ and the concrete principalities and powers
of the time. This does not mean that Barth's account of
the knowledge of God was invulnerable to positivist interpretation, and certainly to positivist use. What it
means is that Bonhoeffer's own movement towards "the
worldly sector"[42] had become so urgent for him that he had
lost sight of the more accurate substance and power of the
KD which was and is that it is not an architectonic com-
pendium of theological loci but a polyphonic description
of the prophetic-apostolic reality to which the Roemerbrief
so powerfully attests.[43] We shall never know, of course,
whether, had Bonhoeffer lived, he and Barth would or could

have corrected each other at this point. Nevertheless, we may perhaps say meanwhile, that the line from finitum capax to religionless Christianity in a world come of age is one indispensable side of the concreteness of theology. At the same time, it must also be said that the finitum incapax is the necessary companion piece if the concreteness of theology, whose concreteness is Jesus Christ, is to be nurtured and preserved from the alienation which could mean the loss of our theological existence today. To put it christologically, where after all, Barth and Bonhoeffer meet and go apart, the vere deus: vere homo must drive us toward and free us for "the man for others"; and contrariwise, the "man for others", apart from the vere deus: vere homo, sooner or later, loses his christological referentiality and becomes some other man.

(3) WO STEHEN WIR?

The debate between Karl Barth and Dietrich Bonhoeffer over the question of concreteness in theology identifies our theological place today. We need not repeat their language but we cannot elude their concern: its focus on the concreteness of Jesus Christ, and the boundaries dialectically drawn by the finitum capax and the finitum incapax; by the vere deus: vere homo and the 'man for others'. There are stirrings beneath the alienation and the secularity of our days which at the level both of culture and of politics suggest that where Barth and Bonhoeffer stopped, we are called to start. The New York Times of Wednesday, 25 October 1972, brought a review of a newly published book by Lionel Trilling called, Sincerity and Authenticity.[44] The thesis is that authenticity has displaced sincerity at the center of the culture and spirituality of our time, and with the dynamics and intensity of a religion. The credo is: "I'm authentic: therefore I am!" It is a piety for the mediocre whose aim is "to extricate themselves from the generality of the commonplace and stand forth in the authenticity of particular being". To this, Trilling's response is that "the falsities of an alienated social reality are rejected in favor of an upward psychopathic mobility to the point of divinity, each one a Christ...". Finitum capax! In the same week, Mr. Anthony Lewis reports that the only wife of a prisoner of war who refused to stand in applause of the recent assurances of the President of the United States of his unsleeping care, was shadowed by an undercover agent who was overheard to say into his "walkie-talkie": "she is now leaving the hall". Finitum incapax! "The Church", wrote Karl Barth, "...has always had to believe in the midst of the world what the world did not and also could not believe".[45] Bonhoeffer concluded his first course of lectures in Berlin with the remark: "our churchly messages are so powerless because they remain always in the middle between general principles and concrete situations. Luther could write the de servo arbitrio and the tract on the tribute money (Zinsgroschen) at the same time. Why can't we do that any more? Who will show us Luther? ...Where is the concrete principle for the demand for obedience?"[46] This open question is our question too. So also is our search for a faith for being human and for resistance in the struggle against the mounting arrogance and brutality of power. Perhaps these reflections upon Barth and Bonhoeffer over the question of concreteness in theology may quicken us to join them in their resolve and at our concrete place, where we are called to be. As Barth so humanly put it: "Die Welt liegt im Argen, aber nicht war, wir wollen uns die Pfeife auf keinen Fall ausgehen lassen."[47] Perhaps the time is coming and now is (to borrow a familiar phrase) when Canada and her churches and theologians will be called to be to the United States as the United States was to Germany in the decade and a half from 1930 - 1945. Refugium et virtus in statu confessionis libertate Evangeliique humanitas humanorum.[48]

NOTES

1 The New English Bible says: "God loved the world so much that he gave his only Son, that everyone who has faith in him may not die but have eternal life."
2 Cf. Karl Barth, Die kirchliche Dogmatik, II/1, par.28. The paragraph is entitled: "Gottes Sein als der Liebende in der Freiheit", which I have ventured to translate as above, in some attempt to take account of the dynamics of God's reality (Being) in action (esse in actu).
3 Karl Barth, Ibid., p. 309; Eng. p. 275. The Vulgate reads at John 3:16: Sic enim Deus dilexit mundum, ut omnis qui credit in erum, non pereat, sed habeat vitam aeternam. The Greek text reads:

οὕτως γὰρ ἠγάπησεν ὁ θεὸς τὸν κόσμον, ὥστε τὸν υἱὸν τὸν μονογενῆ ἔδωκεν, ἵνα πᾶς ὁ πιστεύων εἰς αὐτὸν μὴ ἀπόληται ἀλλ' ἔχῃ ζωὴν αἰώνιον.
As for verse 21, the Greek text reads:
ὁ δὲ ποιῶν τὴν ἀλήθειαν ἔρχεται πρὸς τὸ φῶς, ἵνα φανερωθῇ αὐτοῦ τὰ ἔργα ὅτι ἐν θεῷ ἐστιν εἰργασμένα.
and the Vulgate says: qui autem facit veritatem, venit ad lucem, ut manifestentur opera eius, quia in Deo sunt facta.

4   Cf. Dietrich Bonhoeffer, Gesammelte Schriften, Bd. III, herausgegeben von Eberhard Bethge, Muenchen, Kaiser, 1960, p. 452. Translation mine. Owing to the elision, I have altered the text slightly, without, however, changing Bonhoeffer's meaning. The passage comes from an essay on "The Lutheran Confessional Writings", with special reference to Baptism. Bonhoeffer had been asked by the Council of Brethren of the Confessing Church to deal with this question in view of a tract on Adult Baptism, published by a Silesian Pastor, Arnold Hitzer.

5   Dietrich Bonhoeffer, Gesammelte Schriften, Bd. II, herausgegeben von Eberhard Bethge, Muenchen, Kaiser, 1959, p. 324. Translation mine. The passage comes from an address given at a conference in Pomerania, to the illegal group known as "junge Brueder". The date was 26 October 1938. The subject was: "Our Way According to the Testimony of the Bible" (Unser Weg nach dem Zeugnis der Schrift.)

6   Christopher Fry, The Lady's Not For Burning, New York, Oxford University Press, 1950, p. 63.

7   Matthew 12:43-45; Luke 11:24-26. RSV

8   Compare the following random sampling from the original text of the Kirliche Dogmatik:

      I/1 -- pp. 141, 145, 155, 165, 262
      I/2 -- pp. 287, 403, 515, 667, 788, 897
     II/1 -- pp. 3, 13, 23, 53, 160, 296, 317
     II/2 -- pp. 2, 165, 226, 271
    III/1 -- pp. 2, 243
    III/2 -- pp. 174, 175, 270, 580, 639
    III/3 -- pp. 32, 216
    III/4 -- pp. 480, 558
     IV/1 -- pp. 96
     IV/2 -- pp. 104, 617

Such a random sampling suggests that a fruitful doctoral investigation of the KD would be the explicit and implicit

references to the question of concreteness in theology,
and their constructive significance and limitations.

9 Karl Barth, <u>Kirchliche Dogmatik</u>, <u>Registerband</u>, herausgegeben von Helmut Krause, unter Mitarbeit von Wolfgang
Erk und Marcel Pfaendler, Zuerich, EVZ Verlag, 1970.
The vivid description of something happening between
Barth and Bonhoeffer and ourselves has come to hand,
as I write. It seems particularly appropriate in this
connection, not only because of the imaginative identification of the intensity and depth of the search for
concreteness in our time, but especially because the
remark occurs in the course of a searching and serious
"Essay on a Sermon" by a singularly sensitive and
knowledgeable preacher and pastor of a christian congregation. Perhaps, we have come full circle; and
where we all are, is where <u>Der Roemerbrief</u> started us
all out a half century ago. "Barth's Der Roemerbrief
After Fifty Years" -- sic! But see, Wallace M. Alston,
Jr., <u>On Discerning Good Faith from Bad Religion</u>, in
Interpretation, Volume XXVI, Number 4, October 1972,
p. 454. Dr. Alston, who is Pastor of the First Presbyterian Church in Durham, North Carolina, quotes Alvin
Toffler, <u>Future Shock</u>, New York, Bantam Books, 1970,
p. 18.

10 As regards the question of concreteness in theology in
the writings of Dietrich Bonhoeffer, attention may be
called to the documentary footnote on the sources of
the Barth-Bonhoeffer relationship in André Dumas, <u>Une
théologie de la Réalité: Dietrich Bonhoeffer</u>, Genève,
Labor et fides, 1968, pp. 21-22. The English translation is by Robert McAfee Brown, <u>Dietrich Bonhoeffer-
Theologian of Reality</u>, New York, The Macmillan Co., 1971,
p. 22. See also, Heinrich Ott, <u>Wirklichkeit und Glaube</u>,
Band I, Göttingen, Vandenhoeck und Ruprecht, 1966, especially, chapters 4 and 6. The English translation is
by Alex A. Morrison under the title: <u>Reality and Faith</u>,
Philadelphia, Fortress Press, 1972. The question of
concreteness in theology is, of course, what <u>Sanctorum
Communio</u> and <u>Akt und Sein</u> are all about; and <u>explicitly</u>,
the <u>Ethics</u>. The best treatment of the question, as regards Bonhoeffer's developing thought about it, is
Eberhard Bethge, Dietrich Bonhoeffer, Muenchen, Kaiser,
1967, <u>inter alia</u>, pp. 228-28, 810, 960-61, 967. The
English translation was published by William Collins
Sons and Co., Ltd., London (1970) and by Harper and Row

in New York (1970). See especially pp. 131-42, 626,
759-60, 765.
11 Barbara Hall and Richard Shaull, From Somewhere Along
the Road, Theology Today, Vol, XXIX, No. 1, April 1972,
pp. 92, 96. Italics are the authors'. Bonhoeffer is
curiously missing from these reflections. Hence one
may be allowed to assume that in the view of Ms. Hall
and Professor Shaull the perspective and direction of
his theological thought also fail to open a road.
12 Frederick Herzog, Liberation Theology, New York, The
Seabury Press, 1972, p. 257.
13 Frederick Herzog, Ibid., pp. 1-3.
14 Ibid., p. 2.
15 Barbara Hall and Richard Shaull, Op. cit., p. 97.
16 Frederick Herzog, Op. cit., pp. ix-x.
17 The Random House Dictionary, Unabridged, New York,
Random House, 1967, p. 305.
18 A brief account of the controversy between Piaget and
Brunner appeared on the first page of the second section of the New York Times of Friday, 20 October, 1972.
On the syntactical controversy with Noam Chomsky, see
the New York Review of Books, Volume xviii, no. 12,
June 29, 1972, the article by John Searle: Chomsky's
Revolution in Linguistics.
19 Cf. Karl Barth, Der Roemerbrief, 5te Auflage, Muenchen,
Chr. Kaiser, 1929.
"Was sollen wir nun sagen? Sachlicherweise mussten wir,
im Gegensatz zu den ueblichen schnellen und direkten
Anklagen gegen die Kirche bisher einfach von ihrer Not
reden. ... Die Erkennenden haben neben sich die Nicht-
erkenndenden, die Kinder Gottes die Weltleute, die
Heiligen die Unheiligen." (pp. 346-347; Eng., p. 362-63).
"Den Schluss der paulinischen 'Ermahnung' und damit der
paulinischen Mitteilung ueberhaupt bildet eine Warnung,
gerichtet an die Adresse aller derer, die sich nun
vielleicht -- einverstanden und in ihren eigenen Ged-
anken bestaetigt fuehlen sollten. ... Wer wagt es die
Freiheit nicht nur zu denken, sondern im Hinblick auf
die Freiheit zu leben?" (p. 487; italics Barth's; Eng.,
p. 502-03).
Cf. also, Dietrich Bonhoeffer, Ethik, siebente Auflage,
Zusammengestellt und herausgegeben von Eberhard Bethge,
Muenchen, Chr. Kaiser, 1966.
"Nur selten mag eine Generation jeder theoretischen und
programmatischen Ethik so uninteressiert gegenuebergest-

73

anden haben wie die unsere. ... Das hat seinen Grund
nicht etwa in einer ethischen Indifferenz unserer Zeit,
sondern gerade umgekehrt in einer bisher in der abend-
laendischen Geschichte nie dagewesenen Bedraengnis durch
die Fuelle der Wirklichkeit konkreter ethischer Fragen."
(p. 68; Eng., p. 64).
"Die Struktur des verantwortlichen Lebens ist durch ein
doppeltes bestimmt: durch die Bindung des Lebens an
Mensch und Gott und durch die Freiheit des eigenen
Lebens. ... Ohne diese Bindung und ohne diese Freiheit gibt es keine Verantwortung ... Die Bindung
traegt die Gestalt der Stellvertretung und der Wirk-
lichkeitsgemaessheit, die Freiheit erweist sich in der
Selbstpruefung des Lebens und Handelns und im Wagnis
der konkreten Entscheidung." (p. 238; Eng., p. 224)
Italics Bonhoeffer's.

20 Karl Barth, Der Roemerbrief, op. cit., pp. 3-7, Eng.,
    pp. 27-32.
21 So Dietrich Bonhoeffer, Ethics, based on the sixth
    German edition, New York, The Macmillan Co., 1963,
    p. 88.
22 Karl Barth, Op. cit., pp. 459ff., 475ff., Eng., pp.
    475ff., 492ff.
23 Karl Barth, Ibid., p. 5, Eng., p. 29.
24 See Karl Barth, KD, I/2, par. 15; II/1, par. 27.
25 Dietrich Bonhoeffer, Ethics, pp. 224, 221. The German
    text is pp. 238, 235. It goes without saying, or
    should go without saying that Bonhoeffer uses the
    words, Mensch, Menschen, in the generic sense.
26 2 Corinthians 5:16-17 NEB
27 Eberhard Bethge, Dietrich Bonhoeffer, p. 219; Eng.,
    p. 134. Bethge notes the initial contacts, mainly
    literary, 1925-33. A third period involved the two
    in church-political activities in relation to the
    struggle with National Socialism. It was a time of
    theological distance. The fourth period echoed the
    first, as a period of new questions from Bonhoeffer's
    prison cell, and Barth's posthumous recognition of
    Bonhoeffer's early writings, 1944ff.
28 Eberhard Bethge, op. cit., pp. 220-228; 1054-56; Eng.
    pp. 135-42. The English translation omits the Appendix,
    to which pp. 1054-56 in the original refer. As re-
    gards specific exchanges between Barth and Bonhoeffer
    or systematic comments by each upon the other's
    writings, the most instructive are the following, from

THE CONCRETENESS OF THEOLOGY:

the original texts:
a) Karl Barth on Dietrich Bonhoeffer
   KD, III/1 - pp. 218-21, 272, 277;
        III/4 - pp. 2, 9, 14, 21-24; 460, 463, 513,
                687, 751;
        IV/1 - p. 74;
        IV/2 - pp. 571, 604, 612f., 626, 652, 677f.,
                725.
b) Dietrich Bonhoeffer on Karl Barth
   Sanctorum Communio, pp. 94-5;
   Akt u. Sein, pp. 60-62, 67, 70-71, 74-79, 103-04,
                130-33;
   Widerstand u. Ergebung, Neuausgabe, 1970, pp.
                308-08, 311-13;
   Gesammelte Schriften, II, p. 41; III, pp. 76,156.

29 KD, III/1 (1945), par. 41, 218-21; Eng., pp. 194-97.
   Bonhoeffer's Schoepfung und Fall was published 1933
   (Muenchen, Kaiser); Eng., SCM, Macmillan, 1959.
30 KD, III/4 (1951), par. 52, p. 18; further, 20-24; Eng.
   pp. 17, 19-23. Italics Barth's; translation mine.
   Bonhoeffer's Ethics was first published in 1949; Eng.,
   1955 (SCM).
31 KD, III/4 (1951), par. 55, pp. 460ff.; Eng. pp. 404ff.;
   512ff.; Eng., pp. 448ff.
32 KD, IV/2, par. 66, p. 604; par. 67, p. 725; Eng. p. 533;
   p. 641. This was 1955, ten years after Bonhoeffer's
   execution.
33 KD, Ibid., p. 612. Translation mine.
34 See Eberhard Bethge, Op. cit., p. 223. Eng. p. 137.
   Translation and italics mine. See further, Bethge,
   Ibid., pp. 1054ff. This Appendix material has been
   omitted in the English translation.
35 See Bonhoeffer, GS, II, pp. 286, 289. Bonhoeffer had
   written to Barth from Finkenwalde on 19 September 1936;
   Barth replied from Bergli, Kt. Zuerich, on 14 October
   1936. Bethge records Bonhoeffer's reaction to Barth's
   letter in the biography, p. 223; Eng. p.137. Translation mine.
36 Eberhard Bethge, Op. cit., p. 225; Eng., p. 139. Translation mine.
37 Bethge, Ibid., p. 225; Eng., p. 140. Translation mine.
   The letter is dated, Berlin, 17 May 1932. See GS, I,
   p. 31.
38 See Bonhoeffer, GS, II, p. 289. Translation mine.
39 See Dietrich Bonhoeffer, Widerstand und Ergebung, 13th

75

edition, corrected and expanded, by Eberhard Bethge, Muenchen, Kaiser, 1966, pp. 179, 184; Eng., pp. 140, 144. Translation mine. The English translation renders the colloquialism: "like it; or lump it". The second letter was dated, 5 May 1944.

40 Dietrich Bonhoeffer, Act and Being, London, Collins, 1962, pp. 175-76. German pp. 149-50.

41 See Bonhoeffer's letter to Barth of 19 September 1936, already referred to. (GS, II, p. 285). In the letter to Sutz, Bonhoeffer wrote: "Barth's book on Anselm is a great joy to me... He exposes at last and in a basic way the countless crippling interpretations (Wissenschaftskrueppeln), and shows that he knows exactly and essentially how one can interpret and still remain sovereign." (GS, I, pp. 25-26) Translation mine. In the winter semester of 1932/33, Bonhoeffer lectured on recent literature in systematic theology and there discussed the Anselm book favorably. See, Bethge, Op. cit., p. 1081. This appendix has been omitted from the English edition of the biography. The puzzle is why Anselm did not mitigate the charge of positivism against Barth.

42 Dietrich Bonhoeffer, GS II, pp. 419-21; see also, Bethge, DB, p. 800; Eng. 626.

43 See Bonhoeffer's letter of 20 May 1944, in which the distinction between cantus firmus and polyphony is made, WE, 13th ed., p. 195. Eng., pp. 150-51.

44 Lionel Trilling, Sincerity and Authenticity, Cambridge, Harvard Press, 1972.

45 Karl Barth, KD III/3, par. 49, p. 234; Eng. p. 207.

46 Bethge, Op. cit., p. 1056. Translation mine.

47 Karl Barth in a letter to Dietrich Bonhoeffer, from Bonn, 4 February 1933. See GS II, p. 41. "The World is in dire straits, but we want - do we not? - under no circumstances to let our pipes go out." Translation mine.

48 The allusion is to Psalm 46:1: a refuge and strength in a confessional struggle for the freedom of the gospel and of the human-ness of humankind.

MARKUS BARTH

Current Discussion on the Political Character
of Karl Barth's Theology

I POLITICS IN THE LIFE AND WORK OF KARL BARTH

It is easy to enumerate moments in my father's life at
which he took an active political stance. Also there is
evidence of his interest and engagement in the last and
worst resort of politics, that is, in military matters.
Asked as a first grader in school to propose a sentence
for grammatical analysis, he suggested, "Wellington and
Blücher beat Napoleon at Waterloo." Soon after this legendary incident, the boy began to play enthusiastically with
tin-soldiers, and later he joined a youth cadet-corps.
Eventually, during World War II, he served as a volunteer
in the Swiss army's auxiliary troups. His assignment was
to guard bridges and public utility buildings against potential saboteurs. When he stayed in the United States
in 1962, he was not satisfied with visiting one after a-
nother of the Civil War battle fields and to astonish his
guides by his acquaintance with details of the battles;
he also fired twice a Confederate rifle, and his second
shot did not miss the mark - a coke bottle.
        Still, Karl Barth's engagements in political and social
issues were more permanent than his military exploits.
I will mention five instances:
        1. Between 1911 and 1921, the then minister in Safenwil,
Switzerland, gave the decisive impulses to the first organization of labor-unions in his parish. He gathered
male and female employees for educational sessions in
which he discussed the history of the labor movement, the
plight and right of labor in the Canton Aargau and elsewhere, and the goals, and short-comings of the Religious-
Social Movement, together with the tactics of the Social-
Democratic Party. Much time he spent in cantonal, fede-
ral and international meetings of the groups working for
social progress. He wrote articles for newspapers, gave
public addresses and intervened directly with some of the
'capitalists' in his environment. In about one out of
four sermons of that period he mentioned current political, social and economic issues - always in the frame of
the attempt to explain faithfully the Biblical texts he

had selected. It is, however, amazing that his sermons
on e.g. Amos are not the most outspoken ones. In his
fight against injustice and suffering he chastized the
poor people's drinking and gambling habits as radically
as the exploitation of labor by factory owners and mana-
gers. In 1915 he joined the Social-Democratic party.
Also he pondered for a time whether or not to become a
journalist or run for a political office. However, even
before the Russian October Revolution damped his high
hopes for the establishment of justice and freedom by
political and revolutionary means, he decided against a
flight from the pastorate. He chose to intensify the
quest for the promise, the power, and the directive which
came from a side totally other than politics, trade-unions
or religious organizations. Beginning in 1916, Biblical
exegesis became the instrument and criterion of this
search.

2. When K. B., after the writing and rewriting of a
Commentary on Romans, had become professor in Germany
(in Göttingen, then Münster, then Bonn) he observed with
horror a strong rightist movement among colleagues and
students. On the theoretical level, a halo was provided
for this tendency by e.g. Friedrich Gogarten's theology
of authority. On the pragmatic side, the external and internal difficulties of the Weimar Republic seemed to cry
out for the restoration of the good old imperial times.
Marshall Hindenburg rather than the Social-Democratic
Ebert was elected as Reichspräsident. The German churches
and universities were harbors of conservative thought.
For instance, Günther Dehn, a pastor in Berlin nominated
for a professorship in Practical Theology at the University of Halle, was said to have suggested that a proper
German war memorial ought to show a supersize sugar-beet
rather than a heroic soldier or other symbol, for living
from sugar-beets - this was what the war actually meant
to the German people. Promptly a witch-hunt against this
opponent of militaristic nationalism was started by chau-
vinistic students, and it found wide support or tacit con-
donation among professors, even among colleagure whom K.
B. considered friends. Especially at the Open Forum held
weekly in our home, but also in public declarations, K. B.
sought to change the prevailing political attitude. His
voice could not prevent the appointment of Adolf Hitler
as Reichskanzler. During those years (between 1921 and
1933) wide circles accredited K. B.'s political stance to

78

his Swiss origin rather than to the substance of his
theological work.
 3. It is not necessary to elaborate on K. B.'s resistance against Hitler. Also his influence upon the formation and development of the Confessing Church movement
is widely known. But three things I wish to mention:
(a) The Barmen Declaration, while conceived as a 'theological' document for fighting (Nazi-influenced) heresy
and disorder within the Protestant Churches, became de
facto a backbone of political resistance, as exemplified
by the Confessing Church's Prayer for Peace after the
first Czecho-Slovakian crisis and by Dietrich Bonhoeffer's
participation in an assassination plot. (b) At first it
seemed that the Confessing Church had no other concern
than the freedom of preaching and internal church organization. It appeared to have nothing to say in favor of
the Jews, of ill-treated politicians and of suppressed
minorities. And yet, from the beginning the Confessing
Church was a political factor in Hitler's Germany. The
Nazi regime was quicker to perceive this than were many
devoted church members. (c) The reason for my father's
ouster from his chair at Bonn University was not his
blunt personal refusal to swear an oath of allegiance -
though his qualified refusal was the occasion for his
indictment by state authorities. He had insisted only
upon the right and the power of the (Confessing) Church
to declare that for all German citizens the validity of
the required oath was limited by the contents of the
First Commandment, "Thou shalt have no other gods before
me." During these years the transition from K. B.'s
Christian Dogmatics (1927) to his Church Dogmatics (1932-
67) revealed a change of mind: What had looked like general reflections on the object and substance of faith,
was replaced by instruction on how the church was to give
responsible testimony in the political realm. The church
as the people of God and as a social institution could
not help being a challenge to tyrannical human powers.
It was inevitable that this church should look like a
provocation also to those persons and governments that
were willing to make compromises with the world-view and
new world order represented by Hitler. During World War
II - especially in the periods when Rommel's armies
made progress in North Africa - the Swiss Government was
among those most unhappy with the political implications
and expressions of K. B.'s thought. An opposite position

was taken only by the British Crown.

4. After World War II K. B. was, again, swimming
Against the Stream. However, this time he fought revenge-
ful attitudes toward Germany, the anti-communism which
led to the Cold War, and reactionary political phenomena
in - and outside Germany. He was engaged in this fight
no less radically and eloquently than in his earlier
battle against the religious and political goals of
Hitler. Best known are his report on a trip to Hungary,
his silence during the Budapest Revolt and its after-
maths, and his Open Letter to a Pastor in the German
Democratic Republic. In those years, not only Dulles
and Adenauer, but also theologians such as Emil Brunner
and Reinhold Niebuhr denounced the position taken by
him. As to his private judgement on the theoretical and
practical merits of revolutionary communism, K. B. never
wavered from the sharp criticisms uttered in the second
edition of his Commentary on Romans, esp. in the interpretation of the 13th chapter of this epistle. However,
together with the World Council of Churches Assembly at
Amsterdam in 1948, he acknowledged the concern for social righteousness expressed by the Marxists despite
their questionable accomplishments, and he refused to
give religious sanctification to the superficial or hys-
teric condemnations of communism. The self-righteous
attitude which, with or without benefit of clergy, dominated western churches, democracies, and dictatorships,
was not deemed worthy of theological support.

5. The political character of K. B.'s theology was
finally demonstrated by his attitude to prisoners. His
preaching inside prison walls in a novel tone and language, was accompanied not only by his study for the
whole penitentiary system, but also by extended and frequent private meetings with prisoners. When he offered
a cigar to those he visited in their cells, it was not
to announce the birth of a new baby, but to express his
solidarity and hope. The freedom of God and the freedom of man, these main themes of his theological work,
made it natural for him to work for Liberty to the Captives.

II QUESTIONS RAISED ABOUT THESE POLITICS

Violent opponents, admiring followers, and humble or
cynical bystanders have been puzzled by the ever new

turns of K. B.'s political involvement. Whoever - with
pleasure or dismay - sees a red thread running through
the several phases of his political engagement, faces
questions such as the following:
  1. Are the sketched attitudes and actions of K. B. nothing more than repeated, occasional escapades into
ethical, political, social and other practical realms,
that is, into spheres which in essence are strange and
extraneous to the orthodox core of his theology as it is
revealed in his book on Anselm and in the Christocentri-
city of his Church Dogmatics? An affirmative answer
might include the charge of arbitrariness or ambivalence.
  2. Or, it can be asked whether K. B.'s acts of participation in the political and social struggles of the
various periods was as closely and loosely affiliated
with his systematic, ontological, and exegetical exploits as is application to explication, or, practice
to theory? Those who answer in the affirmative may express their admiration: K. B. did not remain in the safe
enclosure of an ivory tower but ventured out into the
ambiguity of life on the street. But they might also
add the judgement, as does an early book of Charles West,
that K. B., despite all his good theology, was a poor
politician. In consequence, many would ascribe, as
Jesus did in the case of the scribes and pharisees, according to Matthew 23:2 ff, authority only to K. B.'s
teachings, not to the life style chosen and the actions
accomplished by him.
  3. Again, the question can be posed whether serious
and competent political activity is characteristic of
only "the young Barth"? If so, then perhaps the "young"
man can be made to look as attractive as the "young Luther" appears to those bewildered by his later "dogmatical" utterances and stance. Some may go as far as to
consider "Professor Barth" a traitor to "the Reverend
Barth." Others, however, would conclude that the well-
meant actions of the pastor in his theological egg-shells
can and must be disregarded in favor of his more mature
later works. Some may be inclined to consider the later
resurgencies of the old, but primitive political spirit
an equivalent to a relapse into the sins of youth.
  4. The common elements of the mentioned three issues
can be summed up in a fourth question: Is it necessary
and feasible to discover a unity or uniformity that
permeates not only K. B.'s complete theological work,

but also an essential harmony between his teaching, life,
and character? Indeed, it is possible to demonstrate
the unity of his doctrine and life in more than only one
given period, or to delineate the progressive, but logical unfolding of a specific theological topic between
1908 and 1968, or to sketch with love and irony those
personal idiosyncracies that survived or flourished in
the face of ever new situations and challenges. In consequence, many a reader of K. B. makes his choice and
selects the one Barth among the many he does not care
for. However, doctrinal or biographical eclecticism
may not be the wisest or most fruitful procedure. All
too often, not only the critics of K. B. but also those
apostrophiz ed as "Barthians" live from such selectivity.
They seem to be stuck with one single moment, method or
element of K. B.'s work. But is K. B. perhaps taken
seriously then only when the alternative "all or nothing"
is faced and when even in slight details and obscure corners of this theology the unity of his witness is recognized?

III THE SETTING OF A REMARKABLE BOOK

A bold answer to these questions is given in Friedrich-
Wilhelm Marquardt's book, Theologie und Sozialismus.
Das Beispiel Karl Barth's (paperback, Munich: Kaiser,
and Mainz: Grünewald, 1972). Several years ago, the
author introduced himself to the academic public by his
doctoral dissertation, Die Entdeckung des Judentums für
die christliche Theologie. Israel im Denken Karl Barth's.
The dissertation was written under the guidance of Helmut Gollwitzer, a professor at the Kirchliche Hochschule
and the Freie Universität in West-Berlin. Because the
latter was considered not merely a pink but rather a red
theologian, he was not appointed as my father's succes-
sor at the University of Basel. Both Gollwitzer and
Marquardt were and are deeply engaged in the struggle
of the radical student movement in Berlin.
Some additional information about the Sitz im Leben of
Theologie und Sozialismus will facilitate the understanding of its contents.
1. The latest book of Marquardt has grown out of lectures and seminars offered on the excited, explosive
and volatile Berlin stage. While in his brochure,
Studenten im Protest (1968), the author had tried to ex-

plain to bourgeois Christians the motivations of those
students who could no longer pursue their studies as
usual, he now intended to explain to the same students
why K. B., who seemed to belong to the established ecclesiastical and bourgeois value system, is still relevant today. Marquardt is convinced that of all persons
K. B. is the example, and that of all things·his teaching is the stuff which the rebellious present student
generation wants and needs. He expects that even if K.
B. were oversold as a revolutionary socialist, the students would at least begin to read in K. B.'s works and
learn from him how to think in dimensions neglected at
present.

2. The editors of the German monthly Junge Kirche (33,
1972, 2-15) have done a disservice to the author of
Theologie und Sozialismus by publishing his essay,
"Socialismus bei Karl Barth", as late as three years
after it was submitted to them. When Marquardt wrote
this article he was not able to use more than the published political writings of the early K. B. Only later
he volunteered and was chosen as the editor of the as
yet unpublished collection of "Socialistic Speeches,"
which is stored in the K. B. Archive in Basel. Also,
the huge majority of the complete Safenwil sermons were
not yet in the process of being transcribed, not to
speak of piles of other non-political materials dating
from the same period. At any rate, despite the scarcity
of resource material then available to him, Marquardt
elaborated in the essay mentioned on four theses: (a)
"Karl Barth was a socialist;" (b)"the Sitz im Leben of
his theology is his socialistic activity;" (c)"in his
turning to theology, he seeks to establish the organic
connection between Bible and newspaper, the new world
[of God's Kingdom] and the collapse of the bourgeois
society;" (d)"the effect of this turn is the construc-
tion of a concept of God." The article in Junge Kirche
appears to have been written with little care, and to
be dictated by sensationalism. It has not only created
great excitement, but also provoked sharp and well-de-
served criticism. Still, Marquardt himself asks - and
I should like to support this request - that he and his
thesis be not judged on the basis of this article alone.
For his (later) book Theologie und Sozialismus is the
result of much more mature and careful, though no less
passionate and exciting, research and reflection. It

83

may yet have been written and published too soon; Marquardt knew far too little of the total Safenwil activity of K. B., and rules laid down for the post-humous
edition of K. B.'s literary bequest prevented him from
quoting from the unpublished Safenwil materials.

3. Finally, a remark concerning the external, as it
were mechanical, "setting" of the book: the cover of
the paperback. Publishers and author had agreed that
on the front cover a picture of K. B. should appear -
in the company of images of Marx and Lenin. While the
realization of this plan was prevented by the family of
K. B., the previous announcement of the book at the
Frankfurt Book-Show on a poster showing the three portraits harmoniously united, was beyond the family's
veto-power.

IV THE CONTENTS OF MARQUARDT'S WORK

The substance of Marquardt's findings is dependent
upon, and as astonishing as, the hermeneutics used in
his study of and description of K. B.'s work. The author distinguishes between three senses of the writings:
(a) the literal, (b) the intentional, (c) the existential, the latter being deduced from K. B.'s conduct.
Most weight is placed upon the intentionality. Certainly, this hermeneutical method, especially the magnani-
mous discarding of the literal meaning and the context
of many a quoted passage, is fraught with problems.
Marquardt's interpretation of K. B. is so dynamic that
often it looks divinatory, if not arbitrary. But because the eating rather than the preparation of the pud-
ding proves its worth, Marquardt's work and its value
are not only dependent upon its contestable methodology.
I will try to sketch the substance of the book under
five aspects:

1. According to Marquardt, K. B.'s theological work
is motivated by two causes: (a) Left empty and hungry
by the liberal theology he once had ardently studied,
and facing its bankruptcy as demonstrated by the pro-
World-War I declaration of the greatest among his German theological teachers, the Safenwil minister set out
to find and formulate a concept of God that would be
true to God and relevant to the world at the same time.
(b) In seeing the plight of men, women and children in
the factories of Safenwil and its environment, K. B.

84

studied and endorsed the Marxist analysis of the working class' predicament. Dissatisfied with both, the preacherly approach of Hermann Kutter and the political avenue of Leonhard Ragaz toward solving some of the vital problems, K. B. was looking for a new way to call for and establish social justice. In summary, the quest for the unknown God and the concern for social and economical righteousness were the two forces that made K. B. tick. According to Marquardt his question was: is there a supreme logos which controls and possibly brings into harmony the two seemingly contradictory logoi of a transcendent God and of a society immersed in material pursuits? In other words: Is there a way to show that and how the Bible is directly related to the newspaper, that the new world ushered in by God is connected with the need for total social change, and that the re-evaluation of all values includes the necessity of revolution? According to Marquardt K. B. learned to see that the two causes mutually condition and interpret one another. Certainly Marquardt's simplification of these most complex issues and relationships can be considered a sign of primitive, undialectical thinking. But his discovery of vital moving forces may also be interpreted as the mark of a genius.

2. Marquardt discovers in, or ascribes to , K. B. a special method of tackling the two issues before him. K. B. avoids the Scylla of hunting for an abstract theory or ontological system comprehending God or labor, and at the same time he bypasses the Charybdis of engaging in thoughtless, unreflected pastoral or socialistic practice alone. His book on Anselm has nothing to do with the imposition of a philosophical superstructure upon the status quo of societal order. And his activity as an organizer of labor is totally different from a blind capitulation to Marxist theory. Equally, neither the ministry of the Biblical preacher nor the organization of labor-unions was simply identified with the presence of God or the growth of his kingdom respectively. Instead, in successive steps the very being of God was described as a being in action, and God himself was conceived as "the reality that changes all things." Esse sequitur operari (being is the consequence of action) – thus Marquardt formulates K. B.'s emerging doctrine of God, in reversing a scholastic tenet. The active, effective, world-and society changing God displaces all other

concepts of God. In consequence, the theologian can no
longer speak of an aseity of God (God's being himself,
quite apart from his creation and relation to the crea-
tures). It may be remembered that Whitehead and American process-theology argues similarly. Equally, according to Marquardt, K. B. refuses either to identify
process, including revolutions, with God himself, or to
separate total renewal of society from God - as if it
could take place and succeed without him. Instead of
cleverly combining or cruelly disjointing theory and
practice, or, of separating explication and application,
K. B. is engaged in an academically and politically
motivated quest for true obedience to God's will in a
communal life, in line with the order of God's kingdom.
Unlike many philosophers, the theologian K. B., so argues Marquardt, does not intend to interpret God and/or
the world, but to effect change. Since the alternative,
"change the world,rather than interpret it," is also
found in one of the Marxist Theses against Feuerbach,
Marquardt speaks of a fundamental agreement between K. B.
and Karl Marx. In other contexts the author also discovers a consensus between K. B. and Lenin, especially
when the ultimate dispensibility of the state is discussed. Yet Marquardt adds a qualification to this consensus: K. B. stands far to the left of both Marx and
Lenin! What makes the Reformed pastor so revolutionary
that he must be, as Marquardt suggests, counted among
the anarchists? Marquardt argues: While in his earliest
years the Safenwil minister, true to his liberal teachers, attempted to follow or construct a way from the
human yearning and potential to God, i.e. to ascend from
man to God, he learned soon enough that the true way to
know and obey God leads downward, even from God to man.
K. B. discovered that God himself is the arch-revolutionary and his kingdom the source, driving power, and legi-
timization of revolution against the high and mighty on
earth. For this reason K. B. had to fight Feuerbach
who considered God a projection of wishful human thinking
and to reject the bourgeois man-made religion which was
concocted for nothing better than the sanctification of
the status quo. K. B. proclaimed a God who is totaliter
aliter, not in the wake of a lofty theory about a deity
detached from and opposed to societal reality, but because he is the God who changes all things, including
idealistic idols, Marxist ideology, social progress, and

bourgeois fear of radical renewal. Augustine's discovery of the radical change effected by God in the individual soul was transferred by K. B. into the realm of
the human community's material and social existence.
   3. What, then, is the function of Jesus Christ in K.
B.'s theology? Why does his Christology become more and
more explicit and central? Marquardt's book contains
intensive discussions of both, basic Christological dogmas such as the incarnation and subtle dogmatical nice-
ties, among which Cyril of Alexandria's en- and a-hypo-
stasy doctrine and the seventeenth century extra-Calvinisticum rank highly. However, it is Marquardt's bold
thesis that K. B.'s theology is neither a derivate from
his progressive penetration into the mystery of Jesus
Christ, nor the result of the anxiety of the preacher
(Predigtnot) who feels bound publicly to portray Jesus
Christ, and nothing else but Christ. Rather the author
affirms that the discovery of God's revolution, including its acme, the resurrection of the dead and the establishment of God's kingdom on earth, precedes the discovery of Jesus Christ's centrality and the (re-) formulation of Christological arguments. The two causes:
theology and socialism, the two objects of research: the
concept of God and a just order on earth, and the two
resources: Bible and newspaper - all these pairs are
fully present and active in K. B.'s thoughts long before
he confirms and expresses them by Christological references, says Marquardt. The reality and indivisibility
of "two natures" is fully recognized before the exclusive revelation in Christ, or even before incarnation
and resurrection of Jesus Christ are made their eloquent
and persuasive "symbols". Indeed in, e.g. the Tambach
conference, the Church Dogmatics and the Barmen Declaration all emphasis is placed conspicuously upon Jesus
Christ, the church and the Jews. However, this accentu-
ation stems from the search of that which really matters:
justice for the proletariat. Marquardt admits that the
way toward Christology is a necessary feature of K. B.'s
development. But while Christology expresses an ultimate concern, it yet is not essential to the substance
of K. B.'s theology. Essential are and remain God and
the proletariat alone. I will present two examples produced by Marquardt. (a) In his understanding of K. B.'s
references to the extra-Calvinisticum, this doctrine
means that the divine logos is present and works as ful-

ly outside Israel, Jesus of Nazareth, the Bible, the
church, theology, as inside specific forms of his incarnation. Therefore the divine logos in person can be
found in, e.g., the political revolutionary process.
(b) The unity of the two natures in Jesus Christ means
that not only the man Jesus but the totality of the human race and history exists only in essential and reve-
lationary union with God and his will.

4. After the role of Christology has been defined in
such terms, it is easy to state that despite all changes
there is a basic unity in K. B.'s teaching and conduct.
Admittedly there are differences or seeming contradic-
tions between his early liberal and his later biblical
theology; between the first and the second edition of
his Commentary on Romans (ranging from wholesale endorsement of revolution to a revisionist stance, as Marquardt
sees it); between the main foci or pastoral and professorial activities; and between the resistance against
Hitler and the repudiation of anti-communism; between
the voice raised in public concerning world-shaking
matters and the hidden work for prison-inmates. But K.
B.'s theology never pretended to form a solid and tight-
ly-woven system. A fixed definition of a specific concept of God would have been considered by him as idolatrous as an unqualified endorsement of the Russian revolution or its opposite, the Brunner-Niebuhr-Dulles form
of combatting communism. What kept K. B.'s theology together was neither a principle, nor definitions, nor a
position but the way which he had to follow. In his
thought and conduct K. B. did nothing else than follow
the way of God toward man, even the divine inroad into
the disorder of society. This means, according to Marquardt, that every phase of K. B.'s life and every page
of his Dogmatics are equally political. If it is God's
nature to effect total change then a theologian must in
word and deed participate in changing the social conditions.

5. The most radical agent and carrier of God's revolution is the church. When K. B. did not quit the pastorate, when even as a professor he remained a preacher,
when he called his main work Church Dogmatics, and when
he contributed to the foundation and the course of the
Confessing Church movement, he demonstrated that the
strongest witness to God's revolution is borne neither
by passionate individuals nor by the progress of world

history alone, but rather by a very specific society,
the church. Therefore, the ecclesiastic frame and content of K. B.'s theology are totally distinct from political reticence or irresponsibility; rather do they express the conviction that by its existence, constitution,
proclamation and action the church itself is and has
to be a political factor, even "church for the world,"
church for those changes in and of the world which correspond to God's kingdom.

V THE SUM OF THE MATTER

1. K. B.'s life and way, his academical work and his
social engagement are the stuff out of which his theology is made. He produced a Geschichts-Theologie (a
theology determined by and determinative for contemporary history) - though not in the sense of Joseph Hrom-
adka who seemed to identify the finger of God with one
particular form of social change. According to Marquardt, the anguish of preaching, the centrality of
Jesus Christ, and the systematic ontological quest are
incidental to the socio-historical core of Barthian
theology.
    2. Because throughout his life K. B. used two sources
of authoritative information: the Bible and the newspaper, and because he devoted himself to two causes of
equal prominence: the concept of God and the social condition, he ultimately did endorse the intention of "natural theology." Indeed, in Theologische Existenz 1, a-
gainst the onrush of Nazism, K. B. coined the slogan,
"doing theology as though nothing had happened." Admitted also that in the Barmen Declaration, as well as in
his fight against (the Roman Catholic) Erich Przywara's
and his former friend Emil Brunner's versions of natural theology, K. B. rebutted the theory of two sources
of revelation. And yet, these were transitional out-
bursts which later were revoked in the light of K. B.'s
Christological research, opines Marquardt.
    3. Because God is the great revolutionary, and be-
cause K. B. sought to serve this God, Barthian theology
can appropretely be called a "theology of revolution."
This theology is highly recommendable, and maybe indispensible, to all that hunger and thirst for social righteousness.

VI THE FIRST EFFECTS OF MARQUARDT'S BOOK

Theologie und Sozialismus was submitted as Habilita-
tionsschrift to the faculty of the Kirchliche Hochschule
in West-Berlin. By a city-ordinance this equivalent of
a church-related theological seminary was granted the
de facto status of a theological faculty attached to the
Freie Universität of the same city. After examination
of the Marquardt manuscript, the faculty of the Kirchliche Hochschule graded the work as unscientific and
refused to "habilitate" its author as a professor. Upon
this, Helmut Gollwitzer resigned from his professorship
at the same institution in order to devote his services
exclusively to the Freie Universität. Soon after, Marquardt submitted his work to the Freie Universität where
it was accepted and crowned with the author's appointment with professorial rank. Whether the legal steps
taken by the Kirchliche Hochschule against this procedure
will change anything, is not known at this moment.
  2. Marquardt, adorned with a martyr's crown, became
a hero to radical students and professors in Germany, as
well as to many other groups in different parts of Europe. His lectures on the topic discussed in his book
were attended by large crowds and hotly debated. Eduard
Thurneysen was rushed to Berlin in order to clarify disputed points and serve as an arbiter. At any rate,
through Marquardt, K. B. once more became a vital issue
and his dusk-covered books were taken down from the
shelves and re-opened. Especially "the young Barth"
seemed ready for lionizing.
  3. Some opponents of K. B.'s theology felt entitled
to sneer, saying either, "I told you so, now we have the
proof that K. B. was not only an incorrigible Swiss demo-
crat, but even worse: also a Marxist," or, "K. B. has
harvested what he has been sowing. After giving the
devil the little finger, now he is taken in by him wholesale." On the other side, some so-called Barthians fell
silent or cried out in disgust. Unlike Max Geiger in
Berlin and H.-J. Kraus in Göttingen, the Tübingen professor E. Jüngel refused to give an evaluation of the
book to the Habilitationsausschuss of the Freie Universität, and his retired colleague H. Diem wrote a scald-
ing and devasting review in Evangelische Kommentare, ex-
posing above all the ignorance, misunderstanding and
misuse of Christology by Marquardt.

4. In letters, small gatherings and public meetings, a spectre appeared on the wall: the split among the "Barthians" into right-wing and left-wing groups, analogous to the divisions separating <u>Rechts-</u> and <u>Links-Hegelianer</u>. Against the leftist radicals, a party of orthodox interpreters of K. B. appeared to be in process of formation, intent to save the light from the jaws of the communist serpent.

5. In order to discuss the issue, and if possible, to prevent the threatening split, a conference was arranged at which the problems could be discussed in open, thorough and friendly fashion. From July 10th - 14th, 1972, scholars and publishers who had volunteered to edit the post-humous K. B. works - materials for no less than 60 volumes, though not of the size of the <u>Church Dogmatics</u>, are available - met in the retreat center "Leuenberg" near Basel. After current editorial issues had been settled, the editors were joined by other interested and specifically competent parties, and two full days were devoted to the discussion of Marquardt's book.

VII HIGHLIGHTS OF A CONFERENCE

The Leuenberg Conference was convoked and presided by Professor Max Geiger. Professor Dieter Schellong of Münster, Westfalia, spoke on K. B.'s relationship to great issues of the 19th century. Eduard Thurneysen discussed - not without some substantial and pointed criticisms of Marquardt - the way of the early K. B. in the light of his complete correspondence with K. B. between 1913 and 1934, which will be published in 1973, and H. Diem re-iterated his observations on the use and misuse of Christology. During the intensive discussions it seemed as if the theologians present would indeed line up in two arrays, one side dominated by Helmut Gollwitzer and George Casalis, the other by Herrmann Diem and Eberhard Jüngel. However, there were also people who refused to participate in either a beatification or an anathematization of Marquardt - among them Frederick Herzog from Durham, North Carolina, and the professors Kreck, Geyer and Hübner from West-German universities. Scholars from behind the Iron Curtain were unable to attend the meeting.

In quick succession, three events exemplified the existing tension:

1. Professor Casalis (of Paris) gave an unscheduled sermonic speech and said in substance the following: (a) Class struggle is the essence of all history; (b) God is never neutral in this struggle, for (c) he is always at the side of the proletariat and identifies himself with their cause; (d) therefore, only that man is a true theologian who is engaged in class struggle at the side of the poor and needy. At other occasions, Casalis had sought to undergird his stance by a kenotic form of Christology.

2. A discussion of Casalis' challenge was impossible because he spoke no earlier than at the end of a long evening discussion, immediately before his departure. Still, there was time enough for Professor Jüngel to stand straight up and declare, "In the freedom of the children of God of which Paul speaks in Rom. 8, I declare: Ich bin ein Bürger." The last words may indicate a democratic citizen's responsible position and procedure. However, after the Casalis oratory they sounded to some like a confession in favour of the bourgeois class.

3. Certainly they were understood in the latter sense by an American studying in Berlin who on the following morning addressed Professor Jüngel, "How could you, at this moment in history, take the side of the bourgeoisie? I doubt whether it is an exercise in freedom when you declare your solidarity with Nixon's disregard of the poor, the bombing of the dikes in North Vietnam, the belligerent attitude of the Christian Democratic Union in the Bundesrepublik against Mr. Brandt's reconciliatory Ostpolitik." Having heard this attack, E. Jüngel silently packed his brief-case, stood up and left the room, with just a little emphasis on the closing of the door behind him. It proved impossible to make him rejoin the meeting. Thus the "current discussion on the political character of K. B.'s theology" seemed to end in contempt and hatred, a deep abyss appeared to exist between actual or supposed followers of K. B. While earlier verbal exchanges at the conference had been less acerbated, they had been no less grave.

4. However, the conference was concluded neither with a bang nor a whimper. After extremists on both sides had had their say, more moderate voices began to be heard. The cause of the strife in person, F. W. Marquardt, declared his willingness to heed these voices, even at the expense of having to rewrite his book (which is at pre-

sent is out of print).

I wish to conclude my report by listing the most im-
protant contributions, as they were formulated especially by Professor Geyer of Bonn.

(a) In Marquardt's book, again and again historical
observations and theories are converted into dogmatical
affirmations. While recognizing that K. B. was not a
system builder and did refuse both, to formulate a definitive concept of God and to endorse socialism and revolution as such, Marquardt has yet produced a theological-
systematical theory. He might have learned from K. B.'s
own excursions into the history of theology and the
church that the formulation of dogmatical statements
requires more than merely the reproduction of a picture
of the past and present history. A new insight into the
mystery of Jesus Christ himself, based on intensive
Biblical studies, is indispensible whenever theology
shall again become a liberating force.

(b) The tension Marquardt has constructed between an
ontological and a dynamistic concept of God, that is,
the alternative between the esse and the operari of God,
and the search for the priority of the one or the other,
appears to be inappropriate to the praise of God as proclaimed in K. B.'s works. Certainly, if God's nature
(in K. B.'s terminology: his "perfection") is described
by the terms "freedom" and "love", then neither a philosophical ontology nor an existentialistic dynamism, nor
the harping upon the mutual exclusion of the two, can
advance theological research and the church's witness.

(c) The use made by Marquardt of Christological arguments is foreign not only to their biblical basis and
the historical setting of their discussion, but also
to K. B.'s motivation and intention. Marquardt's contention that in K. B.'s theology Christology is no more
than a subsidiary to, and confirmation of, preconceived
ideas and experienced tensions is not at all convincing.
Still, it must be admitted that the acrimonious debate
about Christology at this conference has by no means
brought to light what Jesus Christ really means for the
poor, either in the Bible or in K. B.'s exposition of
the Bible.

(d) Even if it would make good sense to call God the
arch-revolutionary and his kingdom the true revolution
for the benefit of all the world, Marquardt has not yet
shown to what change "revolution" is subjected once it

is taken into Yahweh's and Jesus Christ's hands. Certainly God and Christ do more than merely confirm and endorse one brand of radical political and social thought and action.

Observations, questions and suggestions such as these formed the highlights of the Leuenberg conference. For the time being, they prevented the threatening split into rival factions. They appeared to imply that Marquardt has put his finger upon an essential element of K. B.'s theology: God's revelation in the incarnate logos proves how totally God himself cares for the whole human condition, including all the material and social issues. Revelation by incarnation also demonstrates that theology, together with every other feature of the church's life and witness, cannot help but be political, whenever it is faithful to God. However, the questions posed also included a very critical assessment of the methods and arguments chosen by Marquardt. Above all they showed that K. B.'s heritage requires hard, courageous and productive future work. Instead of giving pat answers it urges the whole church to speak even better and clearer of him who was in Christ reconciling the world.

MICHAEL WYSCHOGROD

Why Was and Is the Theology of Karl Barth of Interest to a Jewish Theologian?

I have been asked to explain why a Jewish theologian is interested in the work of Karl Barth. Implied in that question is a more generic one: why is a Jewish theologian interested in Christianity and Christian theology? Let us therefore start with the genus and then turn to the species.

Since every question proceeds from a frame of reference and is based on some assumptions, it is reasonable to assume that the asking of this question proceeds from some degree of wonder that a Jewish theologian should be interested in Christianity. It has been argued, and there are those who continue to maintain, that while an interest in Judaism is necessary and inevitable for the Christian theologian, a corresponding interest in Christianity is neither necessary nor inevitable for the Jewish theologian. Christianity, we are reminded, presupposes Judaism from which it originated and whose promises it claims to have fulfilled. As such, a knowledge of Judaism is essential for a Christian who wishes to understand his faith. Judaism, the argument continues, does not presuppose Christianity and can therefore pursue its path without much interest in Christianity. While it is, of course, a fact of life that Judaism has, for much of its history, existed in a Christian world and, therefore, been forced into contact with Christian civilization, those who believe that an interest in Christianity is not essential to Judaism consider this relationship a relatively external one, not reaching into the religious center of Jewish faith. It is on such ground that the mild wonder aroused by a Jewish theologian who nevertheless is interested in Christian theology can perhaps be explained. Furthermore, there is the degree of strain that has obtained between the two faiths for some time, a strain that you probably have heard of, and that, too, enters the calculation when this question is considered. In the light of all this, why is a Jewish theologian interested in Christianity? What explains this mystery?

It is, of course, not possible to deny the validity

of the point concerning the a-symmetry between Judaism
and Christianity as regarding their origins. Christianity is rooted in Judaism in a way that Judaism is not
rooted in Christianity and there seems to be no way of
escaping this fact. I cannot, however, conclude from
this that a Jewish theologian, therefore, ought or perhaps even must remain uninterested in Christianity. I
base this opinion on two considerations, both of which,
I think, bear attention by Jewish theology.

First, there is the Divine promise to Abraham that
through his election, or in him, there shall be blessed
the families of the earth (Gen. 12:3). This makes quite
clear that the election of Abraham and his seed, while
in many ways separating the history of Israel from
those of the nations, cannot rest with such a separation.
However appropriate such a separation may be on the way,
in a fundamental sense the destinies of the families of
the earth and that of Israel are intertwined because it
is the Divine intention that the blessing which is ini-
tially Abraham's, in time redound to the benefit of the
nations. Israel cannot therefore be ultimately isola-
tionist, however vital it be that it be so penultimately.
As it pursues its path through history, it expects the
redemption of the nations and watches with great interest those developments which give indication of such a
future. Because this is so, the Jewish theologian can
and must maintain a vital interest in the spiritual life
of the nations with whom it is, in a sense, jointly em-
barked on the path to redemption. It is not to detract
from the centrality assigned to Israel in this process
to emphasize this point. Not to emphasize it is too often symptomatic of a misunderstanding of Israel's election, as if the redemption of Israel could be accomplished alongside the non-redemption of the nations.

But if the Jewish theologian is therefore necessarily
interested in the religious life of all peoples, how
much more must he be interested in Christianity which
has mediated the vocabulary of Israel to all parts of
the earth. At times, I find myself driving on a Sunday
morning in some rural area of the United States. At
this time, as one plays with the dial on the car radio,
just about the only reception available consists of
church services from this or that local church. And as
one switches from station to station, what names does
one hear? David, Solomon, Ezekiel, Jeremiah, Isaiah,

Jesus, Paul and so on, Jews one and all. And what concepts does one hear? Sin and redemption, the Messiah,
sacrifice, the Passover, Jerusalem and so on, Jewish
concepts one and all. And this Jewish vocabulary, this
imagination, these Jewish hopes and expectations issue
from gentile seed, from stock that is not of Abraham,
from people whose forefathers had not been brought out
of Egypt and for whom God did not split the Red Sea.
How can a Jewish theologian not be interested in this?
True, to the Jewish ear there are at times notes that
are not fully harmonious with his consciousness, notes
often disturbing and even strange. But it is not this
that is the wonder. The wonder is that nations not of
the stock of Abraham have come within the orbit of the
faith of Israel, experiencing man and history with Jewish categories deeply rooted in Jewish experience and
sensibility. How can a Jewish theologian not perceive
that something wonderful is at work here, something
that must in some way be connected with the love of
the God of Israel for all his children, Isaac as well as
Ishmael, Jacob as well as Esau. It is this that Maimonides perceived about Christianity when he wrote that
Jesus "only served to clear the way for King Messiah,
to prepare the whole world to worship God with one accord, as it is written 'For then will I turn to the people a pure language, that they may all call upon the
name of the lord to serve Him with one consent'(Zeph.3:9).
Thus the messianic hope, the Torah, and the commandments
have become familiar topics - topics of conversation
(among the inhabitants) of the far isles and many peoples...."[1] Because Christianity has and continues to
play this crucial role related to Israel's mission, Jewish theology cannot fail to be interested in Christian
developments.

My second reason for believing that Judaism should
cultivate an interest in Christian theology is perhaps
less central than the first but nevertheless important.
Christianity is heir to an exceedingly rich theological
tradition. For various reasons, Judaism has not generally invested its most active energies in the theological enterprise. In order to interpret this fact correctly, considerable acquaintance with Christian theology
is required. In the process, the Jewish theologian
learns better to understand the framework of his faith
because he compares it with an alternate strategy, one

that was not taken by his tradition. The result is that
dialogue with a theology as sophisticated as that of
Christianity advances Judaism theologically and compels
it to examine problems it might not otherwise have done.
The danger in all this is that Judaism, by being forced
into a theological mold perhaps partially foreign to it,
is moved toward a self-understanding that is defective
in proportion to its exchange of immediacy for mediacy,
of being for doctrine, of life for thought and of the
Scriptural for the philosophic. But no advance is possible without risk and it should be possible for a responsible Jewish theology to benefit from the experience of
Christian theology and avoid those pitfalls so clearly
marked out by Barth.

Having made these points in defense of a Jewish theologian's interest in Christian theology generally, it is
now necessary to focus on Karl Barth and to ask why he,
in particular, attracts the attention of a Jewish theologian? The answer can be stated very simply. Karl
Barth is the Christian theologian of our time who is
oriented toward Scripture, who does not substitute the
Word of Man for that of God and who does not find himself helpless before the mighty technology of "scientific" Biblical scholarship - an enterprise often replete
will all sorts of hidden agendas not obvious at first
sight. And because Barth is Scriptural, his attention
turns to Israel in a rather unique way which the Jewish
theologian reads with avid interest if for no other reason than the feeling that it was not written to be read
by a Jew, to be commented on by a Jew, to be challenged
by a Jew. It cannot, of course, be maintained that this
is unique with Barth. Bultmann, to mention but one other example, is at least equally oblivious to the possibility of falling into Jewish hands. But then he is so
thoroughly gentile, so Heideggerian, so little humbled
by the so largely Jewish Word of God, that one would not
expect much from him. Barth is different. Because he
is so biblical he is, in some sense, a member of the
family whom Israel cannot ignore.

The first and basic point then that impresses a Jewish reader of Barth is that his faith is not grounded
in some alleged eternal verities of reason or on some
noble and profound religious sensibility that is shared
by all men or by a spiritual elite, but on a movement
of God toward man as witnessed in Scripture. It is of

course true that in this formulation we have omitted the
Christological center without which any summation of
Barth's position is incomplete, to say the very least.
For him, God's movement toward man is inconceivable without Jesus and it is he who is witnessed in Scripture.
The Jewish reader, however, while fully realizing the
centrality of the Christological in Barth, can understand Barth's appreciation of God's movement toward man
in the light of the Word of God which, after all, is also central for Barth, even if not fully equal to the
event of Jesus. The two concepts that emerge as crucial
are therefore the theology of divine initiative and the
theology of the word, both of which are deeply Barthian.
Both of these points are Jewish points. It is Israel
that speaks of its God as He who has brought it out of
Egypt and entered into covenant with this people. It
is not inaccurate to say that Israel's definition of God
is derived from the saving acts experienced by Israel at
the hands of this God. The God of Israel is therefore
the God of Abraham, Isaac and Jacob from which it follows that the God spoken of without the explicit or implicit invocation of the patriarchs is, to Israel, a
foreign God who does not simply automatically coincide
with its God. Barth's refusal to substitute ontological
constructions, whether in the form of the "ground of
being" or any other similar deflection of the God known
by Israel, for the God who acts in Jewish history, cannot fail to meet with instinctive recognition by the
Jewish reader that he has before him a biblically at-
tuned thinker whose focus is on the God of Israel,even
if, at a certain point, the Jewish story diverges from
the Christian. I am convinced that it is necessary to
formulate the matter in these terms, to speak of stories
that diverge, because too often rationalistically minded
Jewish theologians have made it appear that Judaism re-
sists incarnation on some a priori grounds as if the
Jewish philosopher can somehow determine ahead of time
just what God can or cannot do, what is or is not possible for Him, what His dignity does or does not allow.
The truth is, of course, that it would be difficult to
imagine anything further removed from authentic Jewish
faith which does not prescribe for God from some alien
frame of reference but listens obediently to God's free
decisions, none of which can be prescribed or even anticipated by man. If Judaism cannot accept incarnation it

is because it does not hear this story, because the Word
of God as it hears it does not tell it and because Jewish faith does not testify to it. And if the church does
accept incarnation, it is not because it somehow discovered that such an event had to occur given the nature of
God, or of being, reality, or anything else, but because
it hears that this was God's free and gracious decision,
a decision not predictable by man. Strangely enough,
the disagreement between Judaism and Christianity, when
understood in this light, while not reconcilable, can
be brought into the context within which it is a difference of faith regarding the free and sovereign act of
the God of Israel.

Barth's relation to Scripture is the second point at
which the Jewish reader senses a kinship that is crucial.
Barthian theology is obedient listening to the Word of
God. Barth develops his theology of Scripture in the
early volumes of the Dogmatics and while it can hardly
be maintained that Scripture diminishes in significance
in the later volumes, it nevertheless seems that after
the initial discussion Barth does not reopen this basic
issue. In any case, Barth knows what Scriptural authority is, and is constitutionally incapable of imposing on
the Word of God hermeneutic devices derived from alien
loyalties which so often, in other cases, turn out to be
Greek or other gentile sensibilities. The loyalty to
the Scriptural is therefore a spiritual conversion to
Israel's mind, a matter of decisive significance. That
Barth is the first Christian theologian to look to Scripture for his foundation would be impossible to maintain.
Luther and Calvin were also, of course, Scriptural in a
very fundamental way. And yet, there is a difference.
Strangely enough, perhaps it is the historical perspective that any writer in the twentieth century, even one
as resistant to historical relativization as Barth,
brings to his work. For Luther and Calvin it was probably not altogether clear that the Bible was an ancient
document which must be read by means of an attempt to
penetrate the minds of the ancient Jews to whom the Word
of God was addressed. Barth is not primarily a historian; Bible-centered as he is, he is not a Hebrew scholar
(his Greek and Latin are clearly superior to his Hebrew,
unfortunately) and he does not capitalize on the latest
advances in "scientific" biblical scholarship. Nevertheless, there is a very clear recognition of the dis-

tance in space and time between Jerusalem and Basel and
the result of this is that Barth does not carry as much
of his Swiss identity into his work as might otherwise
have been the case. Consciousness of the historical
alone is not sufficient for the achievement of this
attachment to a God who has, as it were, hyphenated his
name to that of Israel so that the two move through history together. This is proven by Bultmann who, historian that he is, also remains splendidly gentile to an
amazing extent. But Barth, I think, does not remain a
gentile, which is to say, he becomes a Christian.
    All of this must not, however, be taken to mean that
Barth's relation to the written Word of God is the
same as that of Judaism. Because he is, in a sense, so
close to it that his distance from it is so apparent.
I know of no better way of illustrating this than by
reference to the so-called Law, the commandments of the
Pentateuch which are the foundations of Judaism. It is
not necessary here to review the Law-Gospel problem in
Luther, Calvin and its appropriation by Barth. After
all the complexity of this issue is taken into account,
after we survey the fulfillment of the Law in Gospel
which is so central to Christianity, the fact still remains that the commandments of the Pentateuch remain
standing, the "moral" as well as the "ritual", and Israel is told time and again that they are to remain
"unto all your generations." Because Israel hears the
Word of God in Scripture it is simply not capable of
dismissing these commandments, whether they make sense
or whether they do not, whether they are in the domain
of morality or even conflict with human morality. Immanuel Kant, in commentating on Psalm 59, 11-14 in
which he finds "a prayer for revenge which goes to ter-
rifying extremes" can dismiss with contempt a writer
who comments "The Psalms are inspired; if in them
punishment is prayed for, it cannot be wrong, and we
must have no morality holier than the Bible" and instead hurl the following rhetorical question which,
for Kant, obviously settles the issue: "I raise the
question as to whether morality should be expounded
according to the Bible or whether the Bible should not
rather be expounded according to morality."[2] Expoun-
ding the Bible according to morality, the choice of
Kant, is surely the antithesis of everything Barth believes, a form of natural ethics corresponding to that

other error, natural theology. The Jewish reader
therefore dreams of a Barth who would understand Israel's
refusal to discard its commandments, its stubborn clinging to practices which make no sense other than that
they are written in the Bible which is all we know or
need to know. I have not found in Barth such an understanding of Israel's biblical obedience. Upon more so-
ber reflection, however, that too is understandable.

We must return to Christology. Barth is profoundly
right when he emphasizes so often that the glory of his
God is his making himself humble enough to enter into
intercourse with man. This is the most amazing proclamation of the Hebrew Bible, the decisive difference
that separates it from the Platonic and the Aristote-
lian Godhead. As such, the Christian proclamation that
God became man in the person of Jesus of Nazareth is
but a development of the basic thrust of the Hebrew
Bible, God's movement toward man. And if all this is
true, then at least in this respect, the difference between Judaism and Christianity is one of degree rather
than kind. Nevertheless, even here a difference remains. Without the incarnation, however much movement
towards man there is on the part of God, there remains
a separation between them which is decisive. If God
became man, the gulf is really bridged, the natures
joined if not fused, the incommensurable made commensurable. And if this is so, there can be no demand
made on man which is alien to his nature, in which
God's demand cuts into the flesh of man because it
comes from Him who is other than man, who, while gra-
ciously having entered into relation with man, is
nevertheless not man but God. The God who became man
commands a being who at least once was fused with God,
which destroyed once and for all the abyss between
them. Israel can therefore tolerate a command which it
cannot understand just because it comes from God who is
not one with man. From Israel's vantage point, the divine command must both reverberate in man's being and
appear strange to him because God has turned to man
but it is also different from him. It is therefore almost necessary, if I may be permitted a forbidden word,
that the divine commandments on the one hand fulfill
Israel's deepest moral being and on the other also sha-
tter it, because God is not man. To the Jewish reader,
it is difficult to escape the feeling that in Christ-

ianity there is a tendency toward the rationalization
of the commandments, though the word "rationalization"
might not be the best possible. In any case, it is a
tendency to make the commandments spiritually compre-
hensible as in Jesus' contention that (Mark 2:27) "The
sabbath was made for man, and not man for the sabbath,"
a remark which directs attention to the recipient of
the sabbath rather than to its originator. For the Jew,
while the sabbath was given to Israel, it is commanded
by God who is not commensurable with man and whose demands need not always "make sense" to man. In fact,
any system of demands which fully made sense to man
might likely be the work of his hands rather than the
Word of God. It seems to me, therefore, that in this
respect Judaism is more Barthian than Barth - a possibility that, I hope, will not strike you as just too
funny.

The proximity and distance between Israel and God is
expressed most forcefully in rabbinic literature in the
duality of God's attributes of Law (Din) and Mercy (Ra-
chamim). At times God acts in accordance with law, as
the judge who metes out to each what he deserves. At
other times he acts in accordance with mercy, cancel-
ling deserved condemnation and awarding undeserved re-
wards. The Jew is fully aware that no man can pass
muster before God if he rests his case on law, on what
he deserves, rather than the unmerited mercy of God.
"Not because of our righteousness," explains the daily
morning liturgy, "do we lay our supplication before
thee, but because of thine abundant mercies." Paul's
polemic against justification by law is therefore hardly an attack on Judaism, as if the Jew felt no need
for the mercy of God but rested his case on what was
coming to him under the law! No thought could be more
alien to Israel. Without God's mercy man is hopeless-
ly lost in his sin, in his guilt before God. But while
God's mercy can be beseeched, it cannot be guaranteed
because, however terrible for man to contemplate, at
times God does mete out justice. If mercy corresponds
to God's proximity and law to his remoteness, then Judaism sees an alternation which it cannot control.
True, in some ultimate sense God's mercy exceeds his
justice, his reconciliation with Israel will be forever while his remoteness is only temporary. But in
the pre-redeemed time the wrath of God is felt by Is-

rael as the deserved chastisement of the people whom
God loves above all others.

For Christianity, things are otherwise. Before
Christ, Paul seems to think, there was law and mercy
and one could never know which would rule at any given
moment. If anything, it was law that predominated.
With the coming of Christ, there is a permanent and
fundamental change. Jesus is equated with the divine
attribute of mercy so that those who believe in him,
permanently escape the danger of standing in the relationship of law to God. In Christ, the attribute of
mercy (Midas Horachamim) has once and for all triumphed
which means that the believer has now escaped the possibility of encountering the justice of God, of being
judged according to the law, according to what he deserves. The Christological event is therefore the final drawing together of God and man, their final reconciliation.

In the later volumes of the Dogmatics, this reconciliation also triumphs in the theology of Barth. His
divergence from Calvin in the rigors of predestination
is rooted in the reconciliation that is the event of
Jesus Christ. And just as the proximity to God erased
those features of the law that were incommensurable
with the understanding of man, so the proximity to God,
the incarnation, makes possible the triumph of mercy
and the permanent calming of the fear of those who,
while praying for the mercy of God, know that God is
sovereign, that His love cannot be fathomed by man and
that therefore His wrath, His deserved wrath, cannot be
excluded as a possibility. I have often wondered why
the House of Israel whose intimacy with the God of Abraham cannot, after all, be paralleled by any other
people, can live with this proximity and remoteness,
this possibility of wrath together with the certainty
of love, while the gentiles who draw near to the God
of Abraham cannot bear his wrath, only his more fundamental love. Perhaps the answer is that toward the
natural son, the father can afford to lose his temper
because there is a security that cannot be shaken.
The adopted son must be dealt with more carefully,
with greater love, because there is less security, less
certainty of the love of the father, a lingering remoteness that must be fought by a greater proximity.
If this is so, then the wrath of God is Israel's sign

of sonship, of its being the first-born, the caressed
son of election. But the gentiles in Christ are also
loved and in time will also be worthy of his wrath.

It is now possible to turn to the final topic that
requires discussion if you are to understand at all
why a Jew is interested in Karl Barth. I am referring
to his doctrine of Israel, a topic dealt with at some
length by Marquardt in his recent study.[3] Given Barth's
attention to Scripture, given his refusal to substitute
human theorizing for the Word of God, it is inevitable
that the Jewish people and Judaism play a significant
role in his theology because they do in Scripture, both
in the Old and New Testaments. But this, of course,
is hardly unexpected or new. Christian authors from
the very first have been interested in Judaism. What
is decisive about Barth is his insight into the status
of the Jewish people after the decisive event of their
rejection of the Messiahship of Jesus of Nazareth.
Very often, the view explicitly or implicitly held was
that, while the Jews had been the chosen people up until Christ, once they rejected the messiah who had
been sent to them, they lost their election and their
place was taken by the church which thus became the
"new Israel", a phrase used as recently as Vatican II
to describe the church. This view Barth apparently
rejected decisively. In 1949 he wrote: "Without any
doubt the Jews are to this very day the chosen people
of God in the same sense as they have been so from the
beginning, according to the Old and New Testaments.
They have the promise of God; and if we Christians from
among the Gentiles have it too, then it is only as
those chosen with them; as guests in their house, as
new wood grafted onto their old tree."[4] In 1942, while
the Jews of Europe were being murdered by the millions
in Europe, he wrote: "A Church that becomes antisemitic
or even only a-semitic sooner or later suffers the loss
of its faith by loosing the object of it."[5] And again,
speaking of Israel, he writes: "For it is incontestable
that this people as such is the holy people of God: the
people with whom God has dealt in His grace and in His
wrath; in the midst of whom He has blessed and judged,
enlightened and hardened, accepted and rejected; whose
cause either way He has made His own, and has not
ceased to make His own, and will not cease to make His
own. They are all of them by nature sanctified by Him,

sanctified as ancestors and kinsmen of the Holy One in
Israel, in a sense that Gentiles are not by nature, not
even the best of Gentiles, not even the Gentile Christians, not even the best of Gentile Christians, in spite
of their membership of the Church, in spite of the fact
that they too are now sanctified by the Holy One of Israel and have become Israel."[6] It may be an exaggeration to assert that statements such as these cannot be
found in the writings of any other contemporary Christian theologians. But if they exist, they cannot easi-
ly be found and, in any case, are probably not as clear
as those of Barth. Barth is thus perfectly clear about
the election of the Jewish people, especially their continuing election after the crucifixion. It will hardly
surprise you to learn that this is pleasing to a Jewish
reader who sees in this a Christian return to its roots
in the faith of Israel.

But this, of course, is not the whole story. Together with statements such as those just referred to,
are others more conventionally Christian and less pleasing to the Jewish reader. Marquardt draws some of
those phrases together from the exposition in Paragraph #34 of the Dogmatics in a sentence all of whose
operative phrases are quotations from Barth's discussion of Jews and Judaism in this key portion of the
Dogmatics:"Barth sagt von der Synagoge in #34, sie
sei die "ungeheure Schattenseite der Geschichte Is-
raels", das "ungehorsame, götzendienerische Israel aller Zeiten", das "nur durch Gottes Zorn geheiligte Israel zur Linken", sei die "Synagoge des Todes", die
zwar "hörende, aber bei allem ihrem Hören immer noch
glaubenslose Synagoge"; sie sei die "tragische, unheim-
lich schmerzliche Gestalt mit verbundenen Augen", sei
"leibhaftig das in Erstarrung stehen gebliebene Alte
Testament an sich und in abstracto", sei die "Organi-
sation einer noch und noch in eine leere Zukunft eilen-
den Menschheit"; sie biete das "Phänomen der ungläubi-
gen", das "Phänomen der renitenten Synagoge", sei
charakterisiert von "hochmütiger Lüge" und ihrem "na-
tionalistisch-gesetzlichen Messiastraum"; sie biete
schlechthin eine "gespensterhafte Gestalt"; ihre
Mitglieder seien "unselige Mitglieder der Synagoge"
und "die Synagogenjuden gehören nicht zu den Gehorsa-
men"; es sei die Synagoge "das unecht gewordene Israel", sie stehe da "als Feind Gottes", habe "an der

Erfüllung der ihr gegebenen Verheissung zunächst keinen
Anteil", habe eine "trostlose Zeitrechnung", lebe eine
"Fleischliche Hoffnung", realisiere eine "fleischliche
Treue gegen sich selbst", praktiziere "jüdischen Starr-
sinn, Trübsinn, Schrulle, Phantasterei" - kurz: sie
biete das Bild einer "halb ehrwürdigen, halb grausigen
Reliquie, einer wunderlich konservativen Antiquität",
das Bild "menschlicher Schrulle".[7] While it is true,
as Marquardt himself admits, that the very drawing together of all these expressions in one sentence lifts
them from their context and conveys a somewhat more
negative picture than is warranted, the fact remains
that Barth uses every one of these expressions in that
paragraph and that no complete account of Barth's position on Judaism can be even provisionally complete without taking this fact into account. What is to be made
of it?

The truth is that Barth's position towards Jews is
ambivalent. Because of the authenticity of his Christianity, because he reads Scripture obediently, he
becomes aware of the centrality of Israel in God's relation with man and in the very message that Christianity proclaims to the world. There is little doubt that
Barth's experience with Nazism taught him just how equivalent the anti-Christ is to anti-semitism, how necessary the destruction of the Jewish people is to those
who make war on the God of Israel and his commandments.
But there is also in Barth an anti-semitism made up of
two parts: the traditional anti-semitism of European
Christiandom (whether the Swiss suffer from this more
or less than others I cannot say) and the anti-semitism
of Christian theology. As far as the first sort of
anti-semitism is concerned, it may surprise some that a
man of Barth's stature is not completely immune to it.
But we must never forget that Barth is also a human being subject to human frailties. In this connection, I
have wondered for years how a man whom I admire as much
as I do Karl Barth, with near-perfection of his grasp
of the evil of Nazism, could have had less than a per-
fect grasp of the evil of that other great war on the
God of Israel, Communism. The only answer I have been
able to come up with is that it was God's way of reminding us that Karl Barth, after all, was only a
human being. The rabbis claim that the reason that
the burial place of Moses was not made known was the

fear that, were it known, it might have become a focus
of worship, with the concomitant danger that divine
attributes would have been attached to Moses. With
Karl Barth, too, in the absence of one relatively major
flaw, there is no knowing what people would have made
of him. It is perhaps for this reason that the vision
in his left eye was not permitted to be equal to that
in his right.

Putting aside the less prominent portion of Barth's
defective attitude to Judaism, the conventionally European
one, we must turn to the far more important aspect, the
theological one. Here the crux of the matter is, of
course, Israel's rejection of the messiahship of him
who is the Lord of the church. This is a decisive matter and it would be ludicrous to minimize the significance of this rejection. In fact, I find it interesting that the church concluded that, in spite of the
fact that a minority of Jews accepted Jesus as the
Christ, it was not this minority that represented the
Jewish people, but the non-accepting majority that did
so. Barth, in close conformity to the tradition, detects a pattern here. Israel, the elect people, is also
from the very first a rebellious people who kills its
prophets, etc. The rejection of Jesus is therefore
very much in character for the Jews who are established
experts in returning disobedience for the unmerited
gifts that God bestows on this people. Again and again
we are told that the record of Israel is consistent: to
return evil for the good of God, disobedience for love,
rebellion for faithfulness.

We have reached a point where I have one confession
and one comment to make. The confession is simply this:
there is nothing more important that I have learned
from Barth than the sinfulness of Israel. There is no
question that the history of the Jewish people is a
history of obduracy and of unfaithfulness. It is a
people that, time and again, has returned evil for
God's good and has suffered grievously for it. I do
not know that this point would be as clear in my mind
were it not for my reading of Barth (and of course,
Paul). It might be surprising that this should require a reading of Barth when this point is so clear
in the Bible. Nevertheless, it is not a point which is
naturally in the forefront of Jewish consciousness and
I am deeply grateful to Barth for teaching it to me.

But, to turn from confession to comment, it is not
the whole truth. Reading Barth, one would gain the impression that there is nothing but faithfulness on God's
part and unfaithfulness on Israel's. This is not so.
"Go and cry in the ears of Jerusalem," proclaims Jeremiah (2:23), "saying, Thus saith the Lord: I remember
thee, the kindness of thy youth, the love of thine es-
pousals, when thou wentest after me in the wilderness,
in a land that was not sown. Israel is holiness unto
the Lord, and the first fruits of his increase, all
that devour him shall offend; evil shall come upon them,
saith the Lord." There is nothing but faithfulness on
God's part but it is not the case that there is nothing
but unfaithfulness on Israel's part. Along with the
unfaithfulness, there is also Israel's faithfulness,
its obedience and trust in God, its clinging to its
election, identity and mission against all the odds.
True, all of Israel's obedience is tinged with its
disobedience but all of its disobedience is also tinged
with its obedience. It is true that Israel does not
deserve its election but it is also true that its election is not in vain, that this people, with its sin,
has never ceased to love its God and that it has responded to God's wrath, to his unspeakable wrath, to his
unthinkable wrath, by shouldering its mission again,
again searing circumcision into its flesh and, while
hoping for the best, prepared for what it knows can
happen again. Perhaps it is not seemly to speak thus,
to praise Israel when it should be criticized. But he
who knows the God of Israel knows how he loves his people and that he loves those who love it.
   To see Barth struggling toward the sign that is Israel, to see him fighting against his Gentile nature
that demands antipathy to the people of election, to
see this nature yield to the Word of God and to Barth's
love for that Jew whom he loves above all others, is
to see the miraculous work of God. The work is incomplete. There remains a dark side, an emphasis on Israel's disobedience which, as we have said, is not the
whole truth. But even more important is this final
point. Whatever Israel's problems with its God may be,
however great Israel's sin and God's wrath may be, the
quarrel is a family one, between Israel and its God,
its father. For strangers to intervene, to point out
the shortcomings of the son, to revel in them, to make

a theology of them, to feel superior because of them, is
a very, very dangerous strategy. However terrible the
anger of a father toward his son may be, it is an anger
that he can afford because underneath it is a love that
is a father's. When others are stimulated by this anger,
something totally different enters the picture and the
father can only be appalled. It is very dangerous to
get mixed up in such family quarrels. He who does, will
incur the wrath of both sides.

I will therefore be frank. It is not for gentiles,
to see the sins of Israel. It is not for gentiles to
call Israel to its mission, to feel morally superior
to it and to play the prophets role towards it. It is
for gentiles to love this people if need be blindly,
staunchly, not impartially but partially and to trust
the instincts of this people whom God has chosen as His
own. If they need be chastized they will be, by their
father who is not fooled. But woe unto those gentiles
who become the rod of God's chastisement of Israel,
the instrument of this anger, the satisfied by-standers
of the punishment. It were better had they not been
born rather than witness this lovers' quarrel.

I have said that it is for gentiles to love Israel.
This, of course, is wrong, it cannot be asked of gentiles. But it can be asked of Christians.

NOTES

1 The Code of Maimonides Book Fourteen The Book of
   Judges tr. Abraham M. Hershman (New Have, Yale, 1949)
   p XXIII
2 Immanuel Kant Religion Within the Limits of Reason
   Alone tr. Greene and Hudson (New York, Harper and
   Row, 1960) p 101
3 Friedrich-Wilhelm Marquardt Die Entdeckung des Judentums für die christliche Theologie: Israel in Denken Karl Barths (München, Kaiser Verlag, 1967)
4 Karl Barth "The Jewish Problem and the Christian Answer" in Against the Stream (London, SCM Press, 1954)
   p 200
5 Karl Barth Church Dogmatics II 2 p 234
6 Ibid, p 287
7 Marquardt p 335. In paragraph 34 of the CD, Barth
   refers to the Synagogue as 'that dark and monstrous
   side of Israel's history', 'the disobedient, idola-

trous Israel of every age', 'the whole of Israel on the
left hand, sanctified only by God's wrath'; he says that
the Synagogue is 'the Synagogue of death' which, yes,
'hears the Word and yet for and in all its hearing is
still unbelieving', is 'the tragic, terribly painful
figure with covered eyes', the 'living petrification of
the Old Testament in itself and in abstracto', an 'organization of a humanity which again and again hastens
toward an empty future'. That organization, Barth states,
is 'the phenomenon of the unbelieving, the refractory
Synagogue', which is characterized by a 'vaunting lie'
and its 'nationalistic-legalistic Messiah-dream', it stands
there like a 'spectral form', its members are 'wretched
members of the Synagogue'; 'the Synagogue Jews are not
numbered among the obedient'. Rather, the Synagogue is
'the debased Israel of the Synagogue', it is seen as 'an
enemy of God', which has 'no....part now in the fulfilment of the promise given to it', going by a 'cheerless
chronology', living a 'carnal hope', taking a stand on
'a carnal loyalty to itself', and practicing 'Jewish
obduracy, melancholy, caprice and phantasy' - in short,
the Synagogue cuts the figure of 'a half-venerable, half-
gruesome relic, of a miraculously preserved antique', the
figure of 'human whimsicality.' (II/2 195ff).

EMILIEN LAMIRANDE

The Impact of Karl Barth on the Catholic Church in the Last Half Century

To my knowledge it is the Dutch Dominican B. A. Willems who, in his small but useful book: <u>Karl Barth. An Ecumenical Approach to his Theology</u>, comes nearest to a general evaluation of Barth's impact on the Christian world.[1] A few particular aspects of the relationship between Barth and Roman Catholicism have been carefully examined. Henri Bouillard has studied the attitude of Barth towards the Roman Church in a very perceptive essay published in 1970.[2] Grover Foley has analyzed with deep insight the Catholic reaction from the theological point of view.[3] My approach, I admit, is different, and as an historian of Christian doctrine rather than as a theologian, I am equally concerned with some of the quantitative aspects as with the qualitative dimension of Barth's impact on Roman Catholicism.

(1) THE IMPACT OF BARTH ON ROMAN CATHOLICISM

Since it is through Hans Küng that Catholic theology was afforded a voice, in 1968, at the funeral of Barth, in Basel, I will take his tribute as a starting point for my address. After mentioning that he had been allowed for the last 15 years to regard Barth as his fatherly friend and constant spiritual companion, Küng alluded to Barth's one time tempestuous relationship with Roman Catholicism: "This may be surprising when we consider that hardly one important theologian of our century has attacked the Catholic Church and Catholic theology as positively, as angrily, and as defiantly as has Karl Barth - in his <u>Church Dogmatics</u> as surely as at the General Assembly of the World Council of Churches in Amsterdam....But his challenge was set forth for all its polemic with that quality which he so praised in Mozart - a great, passionate, free objectivity. And the subject for which he wished to obtain a hearing - a wide hearing - was the Christian message. With the gospel as his starting point, he believed it necessary to speak so sharply, he believed it necessary to <u>protest</u> against us. And he seemed to many of us to be the Protestant theologian <u>par excellence</u>. But actually he protested

not only when he was against something but when he was
for something ..."[4]
   Barth protested for the wholly other living God, for
the ever relevant Word of God in Scripture, for the centrality of Jesus Christ, for the community of believing
men and because of that he has made again Protestant
theology a partner for Roman Catholicism. This is a
momentous affirmation that we may like to hear atten-
tively in Küng's own words: "With his positive protest,
his great evangelical intentions, which must be maintained throughout, no matter what one's position regarding the Barthian system, Karl Barth has again made
Protestant theology itself an earnest, evangelical discussion partner for us Catholics. And with this protest
he has at the same time awakened many of us Catholics.
His prophetic word, also in the Dogmatics, was heard in
our church too, and he himself was surprised how well
heard it was. Karl Barth, precisely as a fundamentally
evangelical theologian in his influence even on the
Catholic Church - very indirect and yet very effective
(and to say this is no exaggeration) - has become one of
the spiritual fathers of the Catholic renewal in connection with the Second Vatican Council, a renewal which in
most recent years often permitted him to ask with mixed
feeling of sadness and joy whether the Spirit of God was
not as much alive in the Catholic Church as in his own."[5]
   I will borrow from these moving comments the main theme
of my address. With Barth, Protestant theology had been
made again - perhaps for the first time since the XVIth
Century - an authentic discussion partner for Roman
Catholics.[6] Keeping in mind the term impact which somewhat includes the idea of influence, but is wider in
comprehension, we will ask three questions in connection
with the fact that Karl Barth has elicited a tremendous
Catholic response: Why did it happen at all?, How did it
happen?, and With which results for the Roman Catholic
Church? Before we examine separately each of these
questions, let us acquaint ourselves briefly with the
very existence of an impact of Barth on Catholicism.
   In his lively portrait of Barth, Georges Casalis,
states that not since Luther and Calvin did Protestantism
have a single theologian of the stature and importance of
Karl Barth, by whose message the Reformed Churches have
been literally shaken. He goes on underlining the different impact it had on Roman Catholicism: "The Reformed

churches have been so utterly shaken by Barth's message,
and the reverberations of his work within those churches
have been so far-reaching, that they have not yet adjusted
themselves to the new situation. ' Like a patient who re-
covers his health very slowly after a critical operation,
they are incapable of analyzing what has happened and of
taking their bearings. Paradoxically - or perhaps very
naturally if the comparison holds - those who are
strangers to the Protestant ethos, for the most part
Roman Catholics, have been much more concerned about
Barth's impact and its implications. The list of works
published by them is increasing all the time, and already
includes a number of works of considerable importance,
making clear that Barth is watched, listened to and understood with real penetration by those outside the circle
of his own confession (he belongs to the Calvinist wing
of the Reformed church), as well as by the larger group
of churches coming from the Reformation itself."[7]   And
Casalis adds a little farther: "If von Balthasar is right,
not only is Protestantism renewed in the process, but the
whole church is likewise affected..."[8]

Karl Barth himself in one of his contributions to the
Christian Century comments upon the decade 1948-1958: "A
special word is necessary concerning what has happened in
the encounter between Roman Catholic theology and myself.
Whatever a man may think about me otherwise, he will have
to grant me the strange fame entailed in the fact that
since the Reformation no figure in Protestant theology
has aroused so much critical but also positive and in any
case serious interest on the part of Roman Catholic
scholars. No doubt the most comprehensive expositions,
the most penetrating analyses, and even the most interesting evaluations of the Church Dogmatics and of the rest of
my work have thus far come from the Catholic camp (with
the important exceptions of the work of G. C. Berkouwer
and that of a young American whose Heidelberg dissertation was recently made accessible to me.) Outstanding
among the Catholic studies is the well-known book of my
Basel friend Hans Urs von Balthasar. And strange as it
may seem in this book the points on which Balthasar and
I agree counterbalance those on which we differ. A most
extraordinary development is the fact that a young man
from Lucerne, for seven years thoroughly trained in Rome
and having become a doctor of theology in Paris, has presented in a book razor-sharp arguments for the thesis

that between the Reformation teaching as now interpreted
and presented by myself and the rightly understood doctrine of the Roman Catholic Church there is precisely on
the central point of justification by grace no essential
difference! So far his book has not been repudiated by
Catholic officialdom, but to the contrary has been openly
lauded by various prominent representatives of that
church. What is one to say to that? Has the millennium
broken in, or is it waiting around the next corner? How
one would like to believe it!"[9]
    After pointing out factors that may indicate that the
Catholic Church was still not determined by its theological vanguard, Barth added: "It remains an established
fact, however, that such a forward-looking group is at
work - thus far without proscription - and before us,
before me especially, lies the attractive possibility, or
rather necessity, of remaining in touch with this vanguard."[10]

(2) THE CONDITIONS OF A DEMANDING PARTNERSHIP

    Let us return now to our first question. Why should
Catholicism to a greater extent than Protestantism be so
obviously interested in seeing anything at all in Barth's
theology? Why did Roman Catholics find in Karl Barth a
fitting, and more than that, an exceptionally admired
and respected partner? We would be tempted to answer
flatly: because he was a real theologian, a great, a
very great theologian, but we have been told that it is
not right for us to declare Barth a great theologian, or
the theologian who was most faithful to God's word.[11]
This kind of sin has, however, been committed time and
again, both by Protestants and Catholics. In the title
of an article of Encounter, Karl Barth has been labeled
"the last great Protestant", and recently a Catholic
writer has called him "a master theologian, the greatest
since Saint Thomas and the only true theologian that
Protestantism ever had". I beg your pardon for repeat-
ing this but I retain that Karl Barth has been accepted
as a partner because he was considered a great theologian,
and not just a great Protestant theologian, a great
Christian theologian, and the greatest of our times.
Balthasar explains that Roman Catholics have learned to
know in Karl Barth a form of Protestantism which has
attained to a genuine Christian Universalism.[12]

You could legitimately suspect Catholic theologians of some haughtiness if they would give to understand that they could accept dialogue only with some kind of unparalleled genius. The fact is that they found in Barth a unique combination of many factors which rendered the encounter possible, attractive and profitable.

The Jesuit Jean Daniélou, now Cardinal Daniélou, really expressed common Catholic reaction when, in the aftermath of Amsterdam, he wrote: "We have loved Karl Barth very much. We are very thankful to him. This is what we have always said and say again. He has rediscovered the authentic value of the Bible. We have loved Karl Barth as the one who has overcome the dogmatic liberalism for which we have not more consideration than he has. And we have loved his tragic perception of the responsibility of the preacher. If we say no to him today, it is with the sorrow of a great disappointed hope."[13]

For Catholics, the greatness of Barth is again, according to Etienne Gilson in a letter written in 1946, "to have affirmed and maintained for our time the unconditional respect of the Word of God," and to "give back to theology its place and its true essence", to "witness so greatly to the vitality of Christianity."[14] We have heard a general answer to our question: Why did Catholics find a partner in Karl Barth? But we have now to explore the matter in more detail. May I first eliminate one factor that I don't consider decisive for most of the period under study. Though Barth has regularly been hailed as a prophet, I submit that the social, political, and even pastoral dimension of his theology which has today so much appeal, have been taken into account rather late.[15] It has not been primarily because of his anxious concerns as a preacher of the Word, nor because of his stand over against the Nazis, that Karl Barth made an impact on the Catholic Church. It is definitely because of his dogmatic theology, as the Barth of the Römerbrief and the author of Church Dogmatics. But once more, let us further ask why?

Catholics have often underlined that Barth's theology represents an enormous step forward as compared to liberalism. An Italian commentator goes so far as to write that: "the interest it has even for Catholics, consists exclusively in its unyielding opposition to liberal Protestantism and modernism, in the reaffirmation of the transcendence of God and of the absolute gratuity of

Grace".[16] The very fact that Barth had forced Harnack to react could only make him congenial for Catholics. But it is certainly not just for this negative reason - Catholics could have found among their own ranks anti-liberals enough - that they became interested in Barth.

A positive factor could be that they found him acquainted with the whole Catholic heritage. As Balthasar noted, "for Karl Barth the history of the Church of Jesus does not begin with the Reformation but with Jesus."[17] For Barth Church Fathers and Medieval theologians were witnesses to the understanding of Scripture and for him the pronouncements of the early Councils were to be taken seriously. A common acceptance of a long tradition has therefore united Barth and the Catholics against pure biblicists. Still in Balthasar's words: "Thus, in Barth's Dogmatics we find a theology that is coextensive with ours in history and subject matter."[18]

If it was not enough to be anti-liberal, it was not enough either to be somewhat Catholic for Barth's theology to be important to the Catholic Church. If his achievement occasioned such a response, it is rather for a twofold reason, according to a statement of Balthasar that has been often repeated: "Barth's work, then, has two features. It is the most thorough and forceful systematization of Protestant thought; and it is the closest approximation to Catholic thought".[19]

Let us take for granted - in spite of some strong affirmations to the contrary - that Karl Barth is genuinely Protestant. According to Balthasar "in his work authentic Protestantism has found its full-blown image for the first time."[20] The problem is really in conciliating this fact with the affirmation that Barth was close to Catholic thinking in spite of his imprecations against the analogy of being, of his stand in regard to philosophy and natural theology, or his frequent polemical anticatholic overtone. While one may speak of "an abyss"[21] between Barth and Catholic doctrine, others, like Edward O'Connor, express more correctly the feeling of most Catholics, when he writes: "Even a Catholic, aware that his own position is probably the chief object of Barth's scorn, can nonetheless sense an accord between Barth's position and certain obscure but profound convictions of his own".[22]

We will see later on how substantial agreement has been claimed on such unexpected grounds as analogy, ecclesiology, and justification. Hans Küng has found that Barth's doctrine on grace is reconcilable with Trent, Fries, that his basic ecclesiology does not warrant a church separation, and Chavannes that his doctrine on analogy is not that far from Saint Thomas. Over and above all agreements on particular points, there exists a common concept of theology. Both Barth and the best scholastic tradition represented by Saint Thomas see theology as a function of the Church, both consider theology essentially within the realm of faith. The very first section of the Church Dogmatics on "Dogmatik als Glaubensakt" is witness to that. We may even say that both also understand theology as a rational pursuit, and Barth has been seen by Catholics as offering a third possibility for modern Protestantism often trapped, to their mind, in a dilemma between religiosity devoid of intelligence and intellectualism devoid of faith.[23] It has even been suggested that if Barth has been criticized for his Catholic tendencies, it is mainly because he wanted to present Christian doctrine rationally and propositionally.[24]

Theology however does not exist for its own sake. Why do Catholics find interest and profit in Barth's theology? An ever recurring answer is that it is because he is the champion of God, of the absolute transcendence of God. At a time of persistent and growing sympathy for immanence and for an anthropological approach, Barth's opposition to all those who, in the line of liberalism, seem to place God in the dependence of man, deserved, for many, unconditional admiration and gratitude.[25]

A few Catholics may have misunderstood the nature of the agreement between Barth and their Church. I don't think that very many have nurtured for long the hope that, like Eric Peterson, Barth would sooner or later join the Roman fold. The agreement nonetheless gave after all some weight to people who assumed that Barth, Roman Catholicism, and the Ecumenical Christianity as a whole were all part of the same diabolical plot.

I do not stop at the Reformation Review, though the phenomenon it represents should not be underestimated by the sociologist or the historian of Christianity, even if it fails to be taken in earnest by theologians. Cornelius van Til, with many credentials, arrives at similar conclusions: Karl Barth, Roman Catholicism and Neo-Protestantism replace the Christ of Luther and Calvin with a Christ "patterned after modern activist thought",[26] their theology is informed "by dialectical principles

that spring from the assumption of human autonomy."[27]
For him Catholic theologians - he discusses at length
Balthasar and Küng - have found a friend in Barth as over
against Luther and Calvin.

(3) THE MEANDERS OF THE DIALOGUE

Looking for the reasons why Karl Barth has become the
partner of Roman Catholicism we have already partly explained how this partnership was established and this
impact made. We must notice that these events happened
in spite of apparently quite inauspicious conditions.
We know how Barth identified Roman Catholicism with the
rationalistic and pietistic trends in part of modern
Protestantism, and how he fought both with equal vigour.
An Anglican writer notes that he suffered "from an in-
credibly ill-considered bias against Roman Catholicism,
which rarely coincides with the greatness of his own
thought".[28] Avery Dulles puts the problem more nicely:
"An ambivalent love-hate relationship with Rome runs like
an Ariadne's thread through his entire career".[29]
I will not dwell here upon the attacks of Barth against
Catholicism and in particular upon his Amsterdam address
(1948) which deeply hurt Catholic feelings and caused
quite a commotion in the Ecumenical world. In a familiar
talk to members of the Reformed and Presbyterian churches
at Amsterdam, he further uttered the following remarks
which may be the most bitter expression of his attitude
during this period: "Do you agree as members of the Reformed Churches to make yours what I was saying to my
Anglo-Catholic friend Ramsay: I am sorry that you do not
detest the pope? I hope that we are not disappointed because a cardinal sent by the Vatican has not come to sit
at the presidential table with Mr. Boegner. Let us not
be sentimental. We cannot associate with the Roman Church.
Things being what they are, the Catholic Church could not
take towards Amsterdam an attitude different from the one
it took. I thus suggest that you renounce the useless
tears that some are tempted to shed because of the absence
of Rome. Where one says not only Jesus, but Jesus and
Mary, where an earthly authority is acknowledged as in-
fallible, we can only say a resolute No. Our only attitude towards Catholicism is mission or evangelization,
not union. Those who know Calvin should agree with me on
this and not hold that it is a Barthian Fancy."[30]

Despite admonitions by dear friends of both camps, Barth gave no immediate signs of repentance. It is reported in his Table Talks that he still said much later: "Roman Catholicism is a terrible thing, because it means the imprisonment of God Himself! It claims to be the possessor of the Holy Spirit and revelation and Jesus Christ Himself. Can there be anything more terrible than the identification of God and man! This is worse than any pantheism! It is the more terrible because it is so pious, so beautiful".[31]

For the consolation of Catholics he added that modern Protestantism was as a matter of fact still worse, Roman Catholicism being at least "impressive and interesting". It is this man who practised no sentimental ecumenism, with whom Roman Catholics thought possible a dialogue that could be "healthy and loyal because clear and sincere".[32] Adolf Keller, writing in 1931 about Dialectic Theology in general, affirms that with Barth (and what was still then called Barthianism), the conflict between Roman Catholicism and Protestantism had entered into a new phase. After the inquisition, the anathema and the practical competition, it has supposedly entered the phase of mutual questioning.[33]

Soon after the publication of the Römerbrief, Barth discovered indeed that his thinking had met with an unexpected consideration on the part of Catholic theologians and it seems that he considered this at the time a mixed blessing. He wrote to his friend Eduard Thurneysen on the 5 of February, 1924: "What shall we say of the three Catholic reviews I received recently, of which each one shows still more understanding than the last? Are these people obeying the secret orders of some hidden Roman propaganda office, which already is speculating on our surrender, or are they the voices of the true Una Sancta we ought to be glad to hear? In any case: we should never stick to a too narrow Protestant perspective."[34]

For the two following decades, the names of Przywara, Guardini, Adam, Grosche, Volk, Fehr, Ries, etc. represent important landmarks. I do not think with Keller, that Roman Catholics have been moved directly to establish a common front in the struggle against secularism and other ideologies.[35] But though denouncing what they consider the onesidedness of Barth in his theology of God and Grace, they acknowledged that a common theological thought was possible. Already for this period prevailed the

attitude defined later on by Hans Küng: "This is not a
business of being for Barth or against Barth. What
matters is the indivisible truth of Jesus Christ ...
Again, we wish neither to write Barth off as a heretic
nor to list him as a crypto-Catholic among our hitherto
hidden assets. In this sense the issue is not Barth at
all - and he would be the first to agree - but the confronting of one another with the mirror of the gospel of
Jesus Christ, in earnest and uncompromising theological
interchange."[36]

We must inquire how this new possibility evolved. It
is really only after the War, when more favourable conditions prevailed, and after the publication of the Church
Dogmatics progressed, that major works began to appear on
Barth, and that different trends became manifest. It is
not for me to decide who have been objectively the best
interpreters of Barth and I can do no more now, than to
point out a few great moments and a few important parti-
cipants in the confrontation between Barth and Catholic
theologians. If we were to select one author and one
book for their significance in this regard we would have
to go back to the decisive contribution of the Swiss
Hans Urs von Balthasar: Karl Barth. Darstellung und
Deutung seiner Theologie, published in 1951.[37] Barth
himself often referred to his shrewd friend from the
other side. Balthasar has seldom made the headlines,
he is no popular theologian, he took as far as I know
no direct part in Vatican II, but he is one of the last
humanists in the great Catholic tradition, an original
thinker, a brilliant writer, an artist. He was the kind
of man who could understand Barth and be understood by
him.

The main intent of Balthasar's book which helped so
much in making Barth's theology a lively issue in the
Catholic Church was to show that about God, creation,
christology and atonement, Barth was in substantial
agreement with Catholic doctrines. Balthasar clearly
explained his initial purpose for the English edition
last year: "We have examined Barth's outlook on nature
and grace and then offered a Catholic Christocentric
viewpoint on the same topic. In so doing, we observed
a gradual rapprochement taking place. This does not
mean that both sides are in full agreement, nor need
they be....

"My book, then, has achieved its purpose. It has shown

that the problems and approaches of Barth are not such
that they justify or necessitate a split in the Church.
Here, of course, I am only talking about the problems
raised in the tracts on God as creator, sanctifier, and
redeemer (de Deo creante, elevante, redimente) not about
the tracts on the Church and the sacraments."[38]

In the meantime French speaking theologians had also
begun to offer their contribution. The first book was
authored by the Dominican Jérôme Hamer, presently on the
Roman Secretariate for Unity. Though probably overly
critical, it was a valuable pioneer attempt at discerning Barth's method and approach. Hamer summed up his
main concern in his original title: "L'occasionalisme
théologique de Karl Barth" which was not retained for
the English translation.[39] It has been claimed that
Hamer was imposing on Barth a straightjacket, transform-
ing a flexible and ever developing theology into a rigid
system.[40] Hamer indirectly answered his critics in the
forward to the English translation, while retaining his
basic reservations. These reservations he worded elsewhere strongly: "The great general weakness of Barth's
theology, even in its most recent expressions, resides
in the lack of consistency it gives to anything that is
human."[41]

A few years later the Jesuit Henri Bouillard offered
us a three volume work which remains to this date the
most comprehensive introduction to Barth and his best
critique, though it still concentrates on the main doctrines connected with God's interpellation and Man's
response.[42] Bouillard had on June 16, 1956, the redoubt-
able honour of defending his dissertation before the
grand jury of the Sorbonne, in the presence of Barth,
reduced to silence by an inflexible protocol.

Bouillard spells out his purpose: "In taking up the
basic problems which are today, as before, the meeting-
ground for the exchange between nature and grace, we
have thought it well to do this in the form of a dialogue
with Karl Barth. There are two advantages to this procedure. On the one hand, the radical position adopted by
Barth demands radical reflection on our part. On the
other hand, because Barth deals in his work with the
whole of the Christian tradition and defines his positions with regard to a number of theologians and philosophers, he affords us the opportunity to envisage the
same problems from various perspectives."[43]

"If we cannot escape debate, we shall not, however, make of it the principal object of our efforts. The angle under which we have chosen to study Barthian thought has led us to neglect (or very nearly) those questions with reference to which the differences between Catholics, and Protestants are most obvious: the structure of the Church, the relation between Scripture and tradition, the understanding of the sacraments, Marian doctrine, etc. Our attention will be occupied with questions of a wider nature which are, generally speaking, situated on the frontiers between theology and philosophy."[44]

Balthasar approves of Foley's characterization of Bouillard's book: "Bouillard has probed deeper into the nooks and corners of Barth's thought, and he has subjected Barth's theology to a thoroughgoing critique. In so doing, he has introduced elements from the theology of Rudolf Bultmann. In the last analysis, however, Bouillard and I are admittedly in agreement on the basic positions concerning fundamental theology."[45]

To hear that Balthasar agrees with Bouillard may be a surprise. As a matter of fact Bouillard probably holds a middle position between the more severe and the more lenient critics. It is the latter who were soon to receive new and strong support.

Just as Balthasar had concluded that the series of problems he had examined were no ground for a split in the Church, a well-known German theologian Heinrich Fries, the predecessor of Küng at Tübingen, brought forth a similar proposition about Barth's basic idea of the Church (excluding of course the particular problems of Church structures, ministry and sacraments).[46] Even the British Hugo Meynell came along the same line at the end of a rather critical essay.[47]

The most influential book for its wide impact on the whole ecumenical scene is Hans Küng's Paris dissertation on justification.[48] It is too well known for me to dwell on its content. Be it sufficient to recall its startling thesis. Within the scope of the question of justification and related problems, Barth has again no genuine argument for separation from the ancient church, or at least an interpretation compatible with Catholic orthodoxy.

The argument was strengthened by Barth writing the author that his position had fully and accurately been reproduced. Consequently, if what is presented by Küng

as Catholic doctrine is really the teaching of his Church,
then Barth admits that his own view of justification
agrees with the Catholic views.

Küng's book has probably elicited more response than
any other comparable theological work. In this manner,
at least, Karl Barth was having a universal impact on the
Catholic world. Nobody writing on the subject of grace
and justification could now afford to ignore Küng and
Barth. Theologians of all schools in Germany, in France,
in Switzerland, in Belgium, in the Netherlands, in Rome,
took sides, most agreeing substantially that Küng had not
only correctly interpreted Barth, but that he also had
correctly interpreted the Council of Trent.[49] Hans Küng
could write in 1964, for the English translation of his
book: "The discussion to date has not brought forth ir-
reducible distinctions between the Barthian and the
Catholic doctrines of justification which would divide
the Church and not just a school."[50]

Balthasar underlined that the focal concern of Küng
provides an even more determined profile of the Christocentric emphasis which he propounded as the proper plane
for dialogue.[51]

Another breakthrough seems to have happened most recently. Henri Chavannes, in a book unlikely to arouse
now as much passion, has conducted a thorough comparison
between Karl Barth and Saint Thomas on the disputed
question of the analogy between God and the world. We
know that the analogia entis has been for a time the
chief heresy opposed by Barth who seems to have confused
the personal·speculations of Przywara with the genuine
thomistic notion of analogy.[52]

As we have seen, although several Catholic theologians
have been laudatory and have endeavoured to find approx-
imations with Barth, most have also formulated fundamental criticisms. They have, on the whole, been strongly
against the so-called dialectic theology and have mellowed
in the measure where they have perceived a real evolution
in Barth's thinking as expressed in the Church Dogmatics.
Hamer, together with the Dutch J.C. Groot[53] have underlined forcefully basic objections to the Barthian system.
For Hamer this system is essentially based upon the actual
and discontinued character of the Word of God and on its
essentially mysterious character, which leads to the
Credo quia absurdum and leaves an irremediable gap between two levels, action of God and action of man.[54]

Henri Bouillard was just as strong about the dialectic period: "God is so totally the unique author of our relation with him that this relation exists only where he limits us, denies us, suppresses us."[55] Karl Barth is seen as more radical than the Reformers in his rejection of man's cooperation with God and this would affect his idea of the Incarnation, of justification, of natural theology, of natural law, of self knowledge.[56] For these critics transcendence as understood by Barth implies an absence of communication.

Avery Dulles has singled out some consequences of this general attitude: Karl Barth was too radical in his repudiation of culture-Christianity, too narrow in his evaluation of other religions, he did not take the historical problem seriously enough, he disparaged the demands of autonomous reason.[57] Yves Congar, a French dominican who has been particularly influential in the context of Vatican II, has also expressed the same very strong reservations about Barth: "While liberating Protestantism from humanistic rationalism, he has renewed and reinforced in it a ferment of heresy the results of which are disastrous. I mean this tendency to consider the sovereign causality of God in God alone, without seeing what reality this causality places in us."[58]

Several watched closely for a further evolution in Barth's thinking. Some found in the 1956 lecture published under the title The Humanity of God the signs of a turning point in his theology.[59] It finally appeared that if there was an evolution still in progress there was no break with the past. Nonetheless the overall image of the relationship of Barth with Roman Catholicism remains that of a positive and mutually enriching dialogue which was dramatically highlighted by Barth's visit to Rome in September 1966.

As far back as 1928, Barth had been aware that in the lower regions of inter-confessional polemics, some of his remarks could be used as arguments for Roman Catholicism. But he had not taken this prospect as an excuse to by-pass the real questions of the Catholic Church.[60]

From the beginning Barth had been concerned with Vatican II and, at the request of Dr. Visser't Hooft, had expressed his thoughts on the Council.[61] On account of his poor health, he had been later unable to accept an invitation to be an observer. But after the cele-

bration of his 80th birthday he temporarily gave up work
on his autobiography to make, in his own words, his
peregrinatio ad limina apostolorum, his pilgrimage to the
threshold of the apostles. He wanted to obtain first
hand information on how the decisions of the Council were
understood in Rome, so he took with him a list of 79
questions which he presented to a series of academic or
ecclesiastical authorities. He even asked the pope if
in the phrase "fratres sejuncti" (separated brethren) one
was to emphasize the brethren or the separated.[62]
Let me quote excerpts from his description of an event
I had personally the privilege to witness: "On the final
day of our stay we had the opportunity to participate in
the International Congress of Theologians who were then
gathered in Rome from all parts of the globe. In the
lobby of the meeting hall we were surprised by a united
choir of young Protestants and Catholics from Wettingen
in Aargau, who welcomed us there in the center of Rome
with Nr. 73 from our hymnal...I was greeted by applause,
honored by a respectful greeting, personally introduced
together with the cardinals who were present... We heard
a lecture by Karl Rahner on the presence of Jesus Christ
in the Eucharist, in which only the frequent use of the
modern word existentialis sounded rather queer to me,
and a discussion led by Professor Semmelroth."[63]
No doubt Barth has been given in Rome a treatment that
would not have been granted to any other scholar from
within or from outside the Catholic Church. This is in
some way a measure of the impact he had made. In one of
his very last statements Barth still mentioned that he
was in very good terms with many Catholic theologians,
at times in better terms than with Protestants.[64] There
was now a sense of belonging together which did not exclude deep searching, but which went farther than just
speaking at one another and even than mutual questioning.

(4) THE MEASURE OF A PERVADING INFLUENCE

How to evaluate the influence of Barth or the effects
of his impact? It would be easy to form a collection of
general remarks like: "Certainly his influence upon
several outstanding Catholic theologians is well known";[65]
or: "The influence of Barth on Roman Catholic world is
great";[66] or: "The influence of that breakthrough has
reached beyond Protestantism into the Roman Church and

bears at least some responsibility for the reformation
which it has been experiencing in recent years";[67] or:
"The pinch of spice that Barth has called his theology
has already considerably seasoned Catholic thought
through Roman Catholic commentators and students."[68] It
has even been suggested that Barth's impact has been more
evident in Roman Catholicism than in much of the Protestant world.[69]

The major question, of course, is whether Barth has had
a significant influence on the Council and its preparation? Avery Dulles answers: "The change in Barth's
attitude toward the Catholic Church should be attributed
not so much to his own mellowing (though he did mellow)
as to the inner transformation of Catholic theology itself in the 1940's and 1950's, partly under the influence
of Protestants such as himself. For alert Catholic
thinkers on the European continent, the dialogue with
neo-orthodoxy stimulated many new insights. Authors
such as de Lubac, Congar, Danielou, Bouillard, Bouyer,
Rahner and Balthasar took very seriously the Barthian
critique of Catholicism. Moving away from the Scholastic
and juridical emphasis of post-Tridentine Catholicism,
they forged within the Catholic tradition a theology that
aimed to be authentically evangelical, kerygmatic and
christocentric."[70]

Karl Barth has undoubtedly helped many Roman Catholics
to rediscover part of their own authentic tradition. An
Irish theologian Colm O'Grady even feels that Catholics
have already listened to the basic positive demands of
Karl Barth: "Barth has contributed enormously to the
recent renewal in Catholic theology, and especially in
its theology of the Church. He epitomizes in fact many
of the advances made by Vatican II. Its primary emphasis
on Jesus Christ and the Holy Spirit in relation to the
Church, its dynamic and joyful presentation of Christian
life, etc., were already his."[71]

If Barth directly influenced Catholic theology, his
impact on the Catholic Church was also indirect but
powerful through the ecumenical movement. Barth was no
ecumenical theologian in the ordinary meaning of the
word, but according to Willems: "When theology really
immerses itself in the mystery of God's revelation and
in so doing invites co-thinking and co-meditating in the
whole of the area of the faith, then it is both Kerygmatic and ecumenical."[72]

In spite of all these affirmations one could yet play
the devil's advocate and question the influence of Barth
as did one writer in 1966: "Still it is true that for
many Catholic theologians, the great majority of priests
and most educated Catholic laymen, the name of Barth
means very little, and the name of Bultmann even less.
This, of course, is even more acutely true in America
than in Europe."[73]

If I try to recall the 50's, when I was a student of
theology, first in Ottawa and then in Innsbruck, I would
be tempted to say that Karl Barth was indeed a big name,
but that he had little direct influence, although I would
not dare to say that he did not have, even then, some
diffused impact.

An adequate survey should cover at least courses given
in universities, and seminaries, dissertations and pub-
lications, and this will probably never be done. For
the sake of curiosity I have looked in the name index of
a few collective works describing the contemporary situation. The two big tomes published in 1957 by the
theological faculty of Milan, with the collaboration of
a wide range of authorities, give an excellent idea of
preconciliar theology. In the index Barth appears among
the authors most referred to, after only Augustine,
Thomas Aquinas and the now already forgotten Dominican
Garigou-Lagrange, those following closely being Pius XII,
Congar, Malevez and Michel.[74]

Fragen der Theologie Heute, published the same year, a
similar though less audacious enterprise conducted by
Swiss theologians and practically restricted to German
speaking collaborators, gives a clear lead to Karl Rahner
and Karl Barth, in the distinguished company of Augustine,
Bultmann, Congar, Cullmann, Luther, Pius XII, and Thomas
Aquinas.[75] A recent Bilan de la theologie de XXe siecle,
a joint project of French and German speaking scholars,
gives Karl Rahner the first rank, followed almost immediately by Barth, Bultmann and Thomas Aquinas, and
then by Augustine, von Balthasar, Congar, Heidegger,
De Lubac, Schillebeeckx.[76]

The influence of Barth in the German language area,
or even in the Netherlands, is almost taken for granted.
I have therefore endeavoured to give preferential attention to those sections of the Catholic world less likely
to have experienced the impact of Barth.

Thanks mainly to the Dominican G. Rabeau and the Jesuit

L. Malevez who quite regularly wrote review articles,
French speaking theologians began as soon as the late
20's and the early 30's to become aware of the importance
of Barth. Early reports may betray an unconscious mis-
trust of Protestant theology but they also give way to
the intuition that something new was happening within
Christianity.[77] In 1934 Yves Congar invited Karl Barth
for a colloquium in which took part Gilson, Maritain,
Gabriel Marcel, Pierre Maury. He himself offered at that
time at the Dominican Faculty of Le Saulchoir, a course
on the theology of Barth.[78]

While the influence of Barth was declining in Protestant Germany after World War II, the interest in him was
rather increasing in France and Switzerland among the
French speaking Reformed. Writing a preface for the
original edition of his book, in 1949, Jérôme Hamer could
nevertheless still write: "Practically unknown in France
until 1933, today his thought distinctly characterizes a
group of Protestant thinkers of ever-increasing importance.
In some measure he even attracts the attention of Catholic
thinkers. And yet, no one familiar with dialectical
theology can fail to notice the superficiality of the
information on a subject that arouses such keen interest.
Diametrically opposed theories are blandly combined under
Karl Barth's name."[79]

The three volume work of Bouillard mentioned before
probably encompasses more of Barth-thinking than any
other work in any language, and has proved too much of
a challenge for translators. Bouillard thus made Karl
Barth really available to the French public who had never
been perfectly at ease with the complexity and abundance
of Barth's writing.[80]

Thanks to the Waldensians, Italy was also early enough
made acquainted with Barth. The first notable Catholic
contribution is the Book of Emmanuelle Riverso which
Barth has listed among the best on his theology. Riverso
felt it necessary to state that "only in Catholicism,
can the vital exigencies of Barthianism have an exact
signification and a true efficacy."[81] Another Italian,
B. Gherardini has written several essays on Barth and
has even at times defended him against those who believed
in the persistence of his actualism.[82]

Spanish language areas had been introduced to Barth by
Ortega y Gasset and Unamuno. Understanding for Barth's
teaching among Spanish theologians went deeper than one

expected and Barth, during his trip to Rome, alludes with praise to the Jesuit Alfaro. [83] Even Portugal eventually heard the good news. [84]

The first significant Catholic study I know in English is from Hugo Meynell, lecturer at the University of Leeds when his book was published. He examined the questions of natural theology, creation, Jesus Christ and human existence, and objected that Barth's emphasis on the absolute sovereignty of God was at the price of human existence, though his general conclusion sounded more optimistic. [85]

A more ambitious undertaking from the British Isles is the study of Colm O'Grady on the ecclesiology of Karl Barth and on the Catholic ecclesiology in dialogue with Karl Barth, first presented as a dissertation at the Gregorian University in Rome and published in two volumes in 1968 and 1969. O'Grady aims at a better Catholic understanding of Protestantism, at an illustration of the actual ecclesiological agreements between Barth and the Catholic Church, and finally at a real dialogue. Accordingly to him the average pre-conciliar Catholic treatise would have very much to learn from Karl Barth, and he tries himself to develop Catholic ecclesiology along the line suggested by him, that is, with an emphasis on the spiritual, christological and Trinitarian aspects. [86]

If we cross the Atlantic we must acknowledge a void which has but very lately begun to be filled. When Arnold S. Nash in his introduction to the Protestant Thought in the Twentieth Century speaks of the supremacy of American influence even in religious matters, it certainly does not apply to our particular field of research. [87] "The American resistance to Barth", the phrase is from Robert McAfee Brown, [88] is an accepted fact for American Protestantism and it is just more true for Catholic theologians. Such a distinguished scholar as the late G. Weigel seemed still to retain, in 1950, a rather negative and, I would even say, primitive view of Barth. Referring to his lectures on the Creed, Weigel makes these surprising comments: "In the light of these observations on the Barthian work it need hardly be said that a Catholic gains no great satisfaction on reading Barth's seemingly orthodox explanation of the articles of the Apostles' Creed. He believes in God, the God of the Bible. He believes that God is one in three persons, though he tells us that this only means that God exists and acts in three ways. Is this fourth century modalism come back to life? Barth insists energetically on the divinity of Jesus Christ, according to the Nicene Creed. He believes in the reality and divinity of the Holy Spirit. Yet all these affirmations - and their sincerity cannot be doubted in the slightest - have as much value as the meanings attached to the words. But such meanings will be expressed by concepts, and toward concepts Barth is rather cavalier."[89]

Weigel affirms that no enthusiasm is engendered in him by the Barthian orthodoxy, for he does not know whether Barth and himself have met the same Christ, but he is rather moved by Barth's singular charm in presenting many Christian dogmas, and by his warmth and rich appreciation of some of their obscurer facets.

Essays collected in 1968 by James F. Andres, then managing editor of the National Catholic Reporter,[90] include only, in reference to the Catholic scene, together with extracts of Küng's book on justification, an appraisal by Edward D. O'Connor of Karl Barth's visit in Chicago, characteristic enough of American Catholics' uncertainty about Barth. Another symptom of the belated interest of English speaking Catholics for Barth is the fact that several of the most significant books on him have been translated only after a number of years, twelve years for H. Fries and even much more in the case of von Balthasar's book about which a reviewer writes that "the mystery question to ask American publishers is why we had to wait 20 years for an English version of this classic evaluation of Barthian thought."[91]

What should we conclude from this necessarily superficial and inadequate survey? That Karl Barth has been so widely read and so constantly submitted to benevolent or rigorous criticism, already implies that he had quite an impact on the Catholic Church. It does not necessarily imply however, that he has had a direct influence, since he could have been studied for the mere sake of knowledge, or just to be more effectively opposed, but this was hardly the case.

Barth's theology has been a wonderful challenge to Catholic theologians. He has forced them to revise their traditional positions, he has made it impossible for them to indulge in the false security of simple repetition. His imprecations have brought them to emphasize or, on the contrary, to pedal down different aspects of their theology. Even the acknowledgement of an approximation with him does not exclude the possibility of some subtle influence. Barth astutely asked Hans Küng what he could have asked Balthasar, Fries, and many others: "May I just whisper a question (a very confidential question..): Did you yourself discover all this before you so carefully read my Church Dogmatics or was it while you were reading it or afterward?"[92] The least we can say is that no close intellectual contact can exist without some form of influence and as Fransen writes about Küng's book, Barth's theology has at least the immense advantage of reminding Catholics that "there are more things in heaven and earth than are dreamed of in our ... theology".[93]

While a number of individual Catholic theologians could have joined Küng in his personal tribute at the burial, or could speak warmly with Bouillard of their personal gratitude towards Barth,[94] I assume that many more could not very well define their relationship with him. I assume that Catholics could produce comments not very different from those collected fifteen years ago in Theology Today.[95] For some, the influence of Karl Barth has been chiefly indirect. He has helped give courage. For many he is the man who has proclaimed the need of returning to the main Christian assumptions (though for Protestants it may mean recover the fundamentals, and for Catholics discard some accidentals), he has been the prophet of God's otherness, of the Christological concentration, of the uniqueness of Biblical Revelation, of faith. He has marked a shift of emphasis from man to God.

CONCLUSION

I assume that most of us do not claim to be prophets nor seers. We can nevertheless inquire, even if with modesty, about the future. As I understand it, a Society for the study of Karl Barth is established, it is anticipated that his theology has a future of some kind. To be honest, at the time of Karl Barth's death, and ever since, this future has appeared grim to many. A. Dulles spoke of the "post Barthian phase".[96] J.C. Bennett admitted that Barth was now virtually ignored in the theological discussion and that even in Europe he had ceased to be the towering figure he was.[97] Ironically, the obituary of the Catholic Commonweal was written by Harvey Cox who observed that most of Barth's thoughts were swimming against the present current.[98] At least two

Roman Catholics have suggested that the answer given by
Barth to Schleiermacher should not be considered definitive.[99]

It has been recently questioned by a French theologian
whether such an admirable (and probably enduring) form of
theology as represented by Barth and his friend Balthasar,
could not in fact precipitate the divorce between faith
and reason. God and the World, Church and history.[100]
This is indeed a concern which does not seem to have
bothered Barth, but which keeps bothering many within and
outside the Catholic tradition.

Balthasar has affirmed that "Barth will never be out of
date for us Catholics so long as we have not confronted
his ideas and found answers for the question he asks."[101]
At the end of the Council it consequently appeared that
the dialogue between Barth and the Roman Catholic Church
would be crucial for the future. It is doubtful now that
these problems will occupy the mind of the theologians as
they did in the past. Re-thinking doctrine along more
biblical lines, as does for example Hans Küng for ecclesiology, may not be the main theological occupation of
tomorrow. Even today Catholic theologians respond as
much to Bultmann, Bonhoeffer or Pannenberg as to Barth.
But who can tell what it will be tomorrow?

Barth once asked the embarrassing question: "Is it so
certain that dialogue with the world is to be placed
ahead of proclamation to the world?"[102] We can only say,
that the trend which finds its voice in the Dogmatic constitution on the Word of God apparently did not take
precedence in the last years over the one manifested by
the Pastoral constitution on the Church and the World.
As a matter of fact Karl Barth has been worried by recent
developments of Catholic theology. Among his questions
about the Council, there was one directly aimed at the
progressists: "Are the adherents of the progressive
majority of the Council...aware of the danger that this
/a renewal in the light of the modern world/ might result in an undesired repetition of the errors committed
in modern Protestantism?"[103] About the trends existing
since the Council he also wrote: "In looking at it we
can only wish that we had something comparable, if it
could avoid a repetition of at least the worst mistakes
we have made since the sixteenth century."[104]

Barth was aware that his questioning could well be
used within the Catholic Church to halt some of the pro-

gressive forces at work. When the editor of the Theologisch praktische Quartalschrift asked him to explain his statement on the progressive Catholics he, on second thought, refrained from it on the ground that it would do no good. He had long made himself clear enough on this point and he was glad with adding these noble words: "I would not like however in the present circumstances to enter as the accusor of my brothers, neither the new-Protestants nor the progressive Catholics."105

A Portuguese eulogist of Barth wrote that there are two categories of geniuses: geniuses of the dawn and geniuses of the twilight: genios da aurora and genios do entardecer, that is geniuses who initiate movements like Plato, Descartes, Einstein, and geniuses who rather sum up or top a period, like Aristotle, Thomas Aquinas, Dante, Hegel.106 The same question has been put about Augustine that we may now put about Barth. Is he for the Christian World in general and the Roman Church in particular, the symbol of a vanishing universe, or is he pointing at a new beginning? Avery Dulles wisely comments: "Only history - or perhaps only the eschaton - will tell us whether Barth's was the last gigantic effort of classical Christianity to assert biblical dualism in the face of modern immanentism and evolutionism."107

We can say no more.

NOTES

1 Cf, B.A. Willems Karl Barth: An Ecumenical Approach to his Theology (Glenrock N.J. 1965)
2 H. Bouillard 'Karl Barth et le catholicisme' Revue de Théologie et de philosophie, 20 (1970) pp 353-367
3 G. Foley 'The Catholic Critics of Karl Barth in Outline and Analysis' Scottish Journal of Theology 14 (1961) pp 136-155; Id, 'Das Verhältnis Karl Barths zum Römischen Katholizismus' Parrhesia; Karl Barth zum achtzigsten Geburtstag am 10. Mai 1966 (Zürich 1966) 598-616. See also, among the relevant literature: A. Keller Karl Barth and Christian Unity (London 1933) 207-224; R.B. Hoyle The Teaching of Karl Barth, An Exposition (London 1939) 48-56; G.C. Niftrik Een beroerder Israëls. Enkele hoofdgedachten in de teologie van Karl Barth (2e ed, Nijkerk 1949) 219-257; K.G. Steck 'Ueber das ekklesiologische Gespräch zwischen Karl Barth and Erich Przywara 1927/

29' Antwort: Karl Barth zum siebzigsten Geburstag am
10. Mai 1956 (Zürich 1956) 249-265; B. Neunheuser 'La
teologia protestante in Germania' in Problemi e Orientamenti di Teologia dommatica (Milan 1957) vol I
616-629; G. Philips 'Trois ouvrages catholiques sur
la theologie de Karl Barth' Ephemerides theologicae
lovanienses 34 (1958) 48-55; J. Hamer Karl Barth 'Introduction to the American Edition. A Reflective
Glance and Precisions' (London 1962) XI - XXXVIII;
E. Lamirande 'Roman Catholic Reactions to Karl Barth's
Ecclesiology' Canadian Journal of Theology 14 (1968)
28-42; S. Ruggiero 'La dottrina di K. Barth sulla
conoscenza di Dio nella valulazione dei critici'
Laurentianum 12 (1971) 65-90, 198-212. Karl Barth has
had few contacts with Eastern Christianity. Berdjaev
has objected to several aspects of his thought. Cf,
Th. Strotmann 'Karl Barth et l'Orient chretien' dans
Irenikon 42 (1969) 33-52
4 H. Küng 'Tribute to Karl Barth' Journal of Ecumenical
Studies 6 (1969) 233
5 Ibid, 234
6 See, along that line: J. Hoffman 'Karl Barth, un par-
tenaire exigeant' Bible et Vie chrétienne Nr 87 (1969)
62-65
7 G. Casalis, Portrait of Karl Barth (Garden City N. Y.
1964) 3
8 Ibid, 4
9 Karl Barth How I Changed My Mind (Richmond Va. 1966)
69-70
10 Ibid, 70
11 H.M. Rumscheidt 'A Thank you for Karl Barth' Canadian
Journal of Theology 15 (1969) 199
12 H. Urs von Balthasar 'Christlicher Universalismus'
Antwort 240
13 J. Daniélou, etc, Gespräche nach Amsterdam (Zürich
1949) 4
14 E. Gilson 'Lettre' Hommage et reconnaissance. Recueil
de travaux publiés à l'occasion du soixantième anni-
versaire de Karl Barth (Neuchatel - Paris 1946) 41
15 Cf, however, H. Bouillard Karl Barth vol I 243-262.
16 B. Gherardini La seconda riforma vol II (Brescia 1966)
189
17 H. Urs von Balthasar loc cit
18 Id, The Theology of Karl Barth (New York 1971) 20
19 Ibid

20 Ibid, 19
21 B. Gherardini loc cit
22 E.D. O'Connor 'Karl Barth in Chicago' J.F. Andrews ed, Karl Barth (St. Louis Miss, 1969) 33 (reprinted from The Review of Politics vol 24, 1962)
23 Ibid, 32
24 W. Nicholls Systematic and Philosophical Theology (Middlesex 1959) 146
25 Cf, J. Hamer Karl Barth (London 1962) 290-291; H. Chavannes L'analogie entre Dieu et le monde selon saint Thomas d'Aquin et selon Karl Barth (Paris 1969) 306-307
26 C. Van Til Christianity and Barthianism (Philadelphia 1962) VII
27 Ibid, 319
28 U.T. Homes 'Barth as Ecumenical Theologian' Encounter 28 (1967) 174
29 A. Dulles 'Karl Barth: A Catholic Appreciation' Christian Century 86 (1969) 408
30 K. Barth 'Les Eglises reformées au sein du conseil oecumenique' Foi et Vie 46 (1948) 495
31 J.D. Godsey ed, Karl Barth's Table Talk (Edinburgh 1963) 43
32 P. Fransen 'Hans Küng on Karl Barth' Month 36 (1966) 42
33 A. Keller op cit, 213
34 Gottesdienst - Menschendienst, Festschrift für Eduard Thurneysen zum 70. Geburtstag (Zürich 1958) quoted by P. Fransen, loc cit, 41
35 Cf, A. Keller op cit, 213
36 H. Küng Justification: The Doctrine of Karl Barth and a Catholic Reflection (New York 1964) XXIII - XXIV
37 A second edition was published in 1962. Cf, W. Kreck 'Analogia fidei oder analogia entis'? Antwort 272-286.
38 H. Urs von Balthasar The Theology of Karl Barth 285-286
39 J. Hamer L'occasionalisme théologique de Karl Barth (Paris 1949) Cf, B. Montagnes 'Parole de Dieu et parole humaine' Revue thomiste 52 (1952) 209-215
40 Cf, J.L. Leuba 'Karl Barth systématisé' Verbum Caro 4 (1950) 182-187.
41 J. Hamer 'La foi comme événement et comme signification. A propos de l'oeuvre du P. Henri Bouillard sur Karl Barth' Nouvelle Revue théologique 81 (1959) 377
42 H. Bouillard Karl Barth (Paris 1957) 3 vol

43 Ibid, vol II p 11, after a partial translation in
Cross Currents 18 (1968) 204
44 Ibid, 16-17 (Cross Currents 207)
45 H. Urs von Balthasar The Theology of Karl Barth 297-
298
46 H. Fries 'Kirche als Ereignis. Zu Karl Barths Lehre
von der Kirche', Catholica 11 (1958) 81-107
47 H.V. Meynell Grace versus Nature. Studies in Karl
Barth's Church Dogmatics, (London 1965) 281
48 H. Küng Rechtfertigung. Die Lehre Karl Barths und eine
katholische Besinnung (Einsiedeln 1957)
49 Cf, B. Willems op cit, 85-92. K. Rahner, among many
others, has backed Küng's main contention: 'Zur
Theologie der Gnade' Theologische Quartalschrift 138
(1958) 40-78; Schriften zur Theologie vol. IV
(Einsieldeln 1960) 237-271. Among reviewers who have
been more critical: J. Ratzinger Theologische Revue
54 (1958) 30-35; B.A. Willems 'Christus und die Kirche'
Trierer theologische Zeitschrift 67 (1958) 257-273.
50 H. Küng Justification XIII
51 H. Urs von Balthasar op cit, 298
52 H. Chavannes op cit, 9, 14-15, 302, 205; Cf, A. Patfoort
'Vers une reconciliation entre saint Thomas et Karl
Barth' Angelicum 48 (1971) 226-232. Much has been
written on the topic of analogy. Among the literature
mentioned by Chavannes, see: K. Hammer 'Analogia re-
lationis gegen Analogia entis' Parrhesia 288-304 in
particular about Przywara, Söhngen and Balthasar.
53 J.C. Groot Karl Barth en het theologische kenprobleem
(Heiloo 1946); his exposition of the Catholic position
has been found inadequate by L. Malevez 'Een recente
confrontatie van de theologie van Karl Barth met de
Katholieke theologie' Bijdragen 9 (1948) 59-71. We
could perhaps list E. Riverso together with Hamer and
Groot
54 J. Hamer op cit, the whole chapter XI
55 H. Bouillard op cit, vol I 26
56 Ibid, vol II-2. L. Bouyer affirmed that Barth was un-
faithful both to the Bible and the Reformers: 'Karl
Barth vu par le Pere Bouillard' Revue des sciences
religieuses 32 (1958) 260-264
57 A. Dulles loc cit, 409-410
58 Y. Congar Chretiens en dialogue (Paris 1964) XXI
Cf, Id, Vraie et fausse reforme dans l'Eglise (Paris
1950, 439-447, 479, 502; 'Pour le dialogue avec le

mouvement oecumenique' Verbum Caro 4 (1950) 120

59 Cf, E. Lamirande loc cit, 38-41; G. Thils 'Chronique
de theologie protestante et d'oecumenisme', Ephemerides
theologicae lovanienses 33 (1957) 511-514; J.N. Walty
'Chronique de theologie protestante', Revue des sciences
philosophique et theologique 48 (1964) 133-134; H. Fries
loc cit, 81

60 Cf, B. Willems op cit, 77-78

61 K. Barth 'Thoughts on the Second Vatican Council'
Ecumenical Review 15 (1963) 357-367

62 Id, Ad Limina Apostolorum. An appraisal of Vatican II
(Richmond Va, 1968) 9-18; Cf, H. Bouillard 'Karl Barth
et le Catholicisme' loc cit, 361-364; A.J.M. van Weers
'Karl Barth Goes to Rome' Frontier 19 (1967) 91-92;
Ch. Journet 'Karl Barth: Ad Limina Apostolorum' Nova et
Vetera 43 (1968) 245-273; R. Marlé 'Les questions de
Karl Barth relatives à la déclaration conciliare sur
la liberte réligieuse'; E. Castelli ed, L'herméneutique
et la liberté religieuse (Paris 1968) 411-424

63 K. Barth Ad Limina Apostolorum 13

64 Derniers temoignages (Geneve 1970) 33

65 H.G. Wells 'Karl Barth's Doctrine of Analogy' Canadian
Journal of Theology 16 (1970) 213

66 W. Dantine 'Ist Barth überholt?' in W. Dantine and
K. Lüthi ed, Theologie zwischen Gestern und Morgen.
Interpretationen und Anfragen zum Werk Karl Barths,
(München 1968) 39

67 J.D. Smart The Divided Mind of Modern Theology. Karl
Barth and Rudolf Bultmann 1908-1933 (Philadelphia
1967) 8

68 C.F. Starkloff The Office of Proclamation in the
Theology of Karl Barth (Ottawa 1969) 136. Karl Barth
presented his theology as a kind of marginal note
(Randbemerkung).

69 'Karl Barth' Christianity Today 13 (1969) 310

70 A. Dulles loc cit, 409

71 C. O'Grady The Church in Catholic Theology: Dialogue
with Karl Barth (London 1969); Cf, H. Bouillard 'Karl
Barth et le Catholicisme' loc cit, 364-365

72 B. Willems op cit, p 76; cf, pp 82-85. See W.A. Visser
't Hooft, 'Message oecumenique' Les Cahiers du
Renouveau Nr 13 (May 1956) 43-43; Id, 'In Memoriam
Karl Barth' Oekumenische Rundschau 18 (1969) 248

73 L. Swidler Introduction to H. Fries: Bultmann-Barth
and Catholic Theology (Pittsburg 1967) 17

74 Problemi e orientamenti di teologia dommatica 2 vols,
(Milan 1957); it is amazing that there is but one reference to Barth in G. Thils, Orientations de la
théologie (Louvain 1958)
75 J. Feiner etc, ed, Fragen der Theologie Heute (Zürich-
Köln 1957)
76 R. Vander Gucht and H. Vorgrimler ed, Bilan de la
théologie du XXe siècle (Tournai 1970); simultaneously
published in German by Herder.
77 Cf, L. Malevez 'Un mouvement recent de la théologie
protestante. L'école de Karl Barth' Nouvelle Revue
Théologique 55 (1928) 650-663; G. Rabeau 'Théologie
protestante allemande' Revue des Sciences philosophique
et théologique 19 (1930) 359-386
78 Cf, Y. Congar Chrétiens en dialogue XX-XXI
79 J. Hamer Karl Barth V
80 B. Willems op cit, 85
81 E. Riverso La teologia esistenzialistica di Karl Barth,
(Naples 1955) 400
82 For a bibliography of the literature on Barth in
Italian, cf, Problemi e Orientamenti vol I 658, and
B. Gherardini La seconda riforma vol II 195-196
83 Cf, B. Willems op cit, 87; K. Barth Ad Limina
Apostolorum 13; J. M. Alonso 'Karl Barth un cripto-
católico?' Rivista Española de teología 17 (1957) 357-
382; J. Alfaro 'Justificación Barthiana y justificación
Catolica' Gregorianum 38 (1958)
84 G. Vagos 'Karl Barth, Professor e profeta' Brotéria
89 (1969) 3-17
85 H.V. Meynell op cit, Cf, P. Fransen loc cit, 42
86 C. O'Grady The Church in the Theology of Karl Barth
(London 1968) 1-3; The Church in Catholic Theology
333-336
87 A.S. Nash:Introduction to Protestant Thought in the
Twentieth Century (New York 1957) VII. The first
book published in America on Barth is by W. Pauck
Karl Barth. Prophet of a New Christianity? (New York
1931)
88 R. McAfee Brown Introduction to G. Casalis Portrait
of Karl Barth XII
89 G. Weigel 'A Survey of Protestant Theology in Our Day'
Proceedings of the Catholic Theological Society of
America 11 (1950) 558
90 J.F. Andrews ed, Karl Barth (Saint Louis, Miss, 1969)
91 M.A. Fahey, Book review America 125 (1971) 18. We

should note that it also happened the other way
around: S. Matczak Karl Barth on God: The Knowledge
of the Divine Existence (New York 1962) was published
in French in 1968.

92 K. Barth 'A Letter to the Author' H. Küng Justification XXI. Cf, H. Chavannes op cit, 306

93 P. Fransen loc cit, 47. Though most Catholic theolo-
gians have dealt with the main issues of Barth's
teaching some have explored such topics as mariology:
A.C. Cochrane 'The Theological Basis of Liturgical
Devotion to Mary Re-examined' in Marian Studies 19
(1968) 49-69 (parallel between K. Barth and K. Rahner);
G. Tait 'Karl Barth and the Virgin Mary' Journal of
Ecumenical Studies 4 (1967) 406-425; K. Barth 'A
Letter about Mariology' Ad Limina Apostolorum 59-62;
Christian celibacy C. Starkloof 'Karl Barth on
Christian Celibacy' Review for Religious 27 (1969)
1089-1096; marriage: O. Wond 'Le mariage dans la
pensée de Karl Barth' Istina 15 (1970) 295-310

94 H. Bouillard 'Karl Barth et le Catholicisme' loc cit,
353

95 Theology Today 13 (1956-1957) 358-415

96 A. Dulles loc cit, 410

97 J.C. Bennett 'Karl Barth 1886-1968' Christianity and
Crisis 28 (1968-1969) 326-328

98 H. Cox 'In Memory of Karl Barth' Commonweal 89 (1968-
1969) 424-425

99 B. Willems 'Barth's abgebrokengesprek met Schleiermacher'
Tijdschrift voor theologie 9 (1969) 2-10; C.F.
Starklorr 'Schleiermacher and Barth on Religious Experience' Revue de l'Université d'Ottawa 39 (1969)
114-131

100 Cl. Geffre 'Declin ou renouveau de la theologie dog-
matique' Le Point théologique Nr 1 (Paris 1971) 47-
48

101 H. Urs von Balthasar The Theology of Karl Barth 19

102 K. Barth Ad Limina Apostolorum 27

103 Ibid, 20

104 Ibid, 17

105 Cf, A. Hasler 'Augustin Bea und Karl Barth in memoriam' Theologisch praktische Quartalschrift 117
(1969) 300, where is reproduced the very interesting letter of Karl Barth. For a local debate in
reference to Barth: P. Hitz 'Actualité de Karl Barth'
Le Devoir January 12 and 13 1970; with an answer by

a group of people involved in Catechetics: 'Réponse a une critique' ibid, February 3 and 4 1970.
106 G. Vagos <u>loc cit</u>, 3
107 A. Dulles <u>loc cit</u>, 410

ARTHUR C. COCHRANE

The Karl Barth I Knew

What sort of a man was Karl Barth? Everyone knows and
remembers another man from his own limited vantage point
and from opportunities for personal contact with him and
his work. I am sure that there are many who are better
qualified to talk about Karl Barth and who have been more
intimately acquainted with him than I. Certainly his son,
Markus, could tell us much more about his father as a
human being. For what relationship is closer than that
of a father to a son, a son to a father? Perhaps wisely,
perhaps for theological reasons, Markus chose instead to
tell us something about the "current discussion on the
political character of Karl Barth's theology." I rather
think that this is what his father would want him to do.
    Frankly I am troubled about talking about the man Karl
Barth. I am not sure that the old gentleman would ap-
prove. You all will recall the tremendous impression
which Grünewald's painting of Jesus made upon him -- of
the finger of John the Baptist pointing to him on the
Cross, of John who said: "I must decrease that he might
increase." The fact is that one can only describe Karl
Barth theologically, that is, in a broken, indirect,
dialectical fashion, not because he was a theologian, but
because he can be understood only in relation to Him who
was "the object of his faith." The Karl Barth I knew was
a man about whom, humanly speaking, one can know very
little. Like Calvin but unlike Luther, Barth rarely
wrote or talked about himself. When he did, as in the
prefaces to the volumes of the Church Dogmatics, it was
invariably in relation to his work in service of the Word
of God. We know little about his religious experience,
and nothing about his conversion. But somewhere along
the line he must have come to the place where he no
longer wanted to know himself or to be known "after the
flesh" or "from a human point of view." From then on he
deprecated any well-meant eulogies. He knew that the
truth about himself is to be found in Christ. Consequently
he consistently directed attention away from himself to
Christ. As early as 1920 he noted "the surprisingly
meager interest of the Bible in biography, in the develop-

142

ment of its heroes. There is no gripping history of the
youth and conversion of Jeremiah, no report of the edify-
ing death of Paul. To the grief of our theological contemporaries there is above all no 'Life of Jesus.' What
we hear of these men they never tell themselves; we do
not read it in their 'life and letters.' The man of the
Bible stands or falls with his task, his work."

So it is with Barth himself. If I may avail myself of
christological analogies, I do not wish to give a docetic
image of Barth, as if he were not a regular he-man. Nor
do I wish to paint a Nestorian picture of Barth, as if his
human nature could be understood apart from Jesus to whom
he sought to bear witness.

One of my earliest and lasting impressions of Karl Barth
is that he was a remarkably unreligious man. He once said:
"I will not build a Christian home." This may sound strange,
coming as it does from a man who had five children, one of
whom (Markus) became a professor of New Testament, another
(Christoph) a professor of the Old Testament. He wrote: "At
the moment when religion becomes conscious of religion,
when it becomes a psychologically and historically con-
ceivable magnitude in the world, it falls away from its
inner character, from its truth, to idols....The polemic
of the Bible, unlike that of the religions, is directed not
against the godless world but against the religious world,
whether it worships under the auspices of Baal or of
Jehovah."

Hence Barth's own polemic was directed against the religiosity of the 19th and 20th centuries. "Can a minister
be saved?" he asked. "I would answer that with men this is
impossible; but with God all things are possible. God may
pluck us as a brand out of the fire. But so far as we
know, there is no one who deserves the wrath of God more
abundantly than the ministers." May I interject that this
aspect of Barth is very relevant today when there seems to
be a resurgence of experiential religion.

On the other hand, Barth was not a secularist or a word-
ling. In his latter years he showed considerable impatience
with those who were writing about "the secular meaning of
the Gospel", "the secular city" or about what "God is doing
in the world." He had no desire "to take part in the discussions of the idiotic 'God is dead' movement, which on
both sides of the Atlantic was showing itself to be the
ultimate and fairest fruit of the glorious existential
theology; and I had even less desire" he wrote, "to take

part in the just as idiotic 'Confessional Movement'" -- a
movement organized in Germany to oppose the former.[1]   The
truth is that Barth saw man, himself included, determined
by an event beyond the dialectic of the secular and the
religious. He saw both the publican and the Pharisee
judged and pardoned by God in Jesus Christ.

Accordingly, the Karl Barth I knew was a humble man. We
must be careful here. His humility was not an innate
quality or virtue for which he could be praised or of which
he could boast. He was humble because he had been humbled
by God. At the celebration of his eightieth birthday in
Basel, May 1966, he reminded those of us who attended that,
though there might be great doctors, scientists and states-
men, there are only little theologians. In an article
written September 1923 he declared: "The greatness of the
fathers lay in their ability to see the gate definitely
shut against all human greatness, and especially their own."
During his visit to the United States in 1962 he was a guest
in our home and met with a group of lay men and women who
had been studying some of his works. One of the group,
then a high school teacher, asked Dr. Barth to autograph
a copy of his little book of sermons, Deliverance to the
Captives. I remarked that a friend of mine had described
that particular volume as "the brightest jewel in his
crown." His reaction was swift and spontaneous: "I don't
like that! I have no crown! I don't like that! I have
no crown!" I tried to explain that my friend simply meant
that this little book was the finest and best thing he had
written. But I failed to pacify him.

At the same time Barth was not given to false modesty.
He was well aware of his gifts and accomplishments, and of
his place in history. For instance, in the foreward to
the last and thirteenth volume of his great work, the
Church Dogmatics, in which he attacked the doctrine and
practice of baptism in the Roman Catholic, Lutheran and
Reformed traditions, he wrote: "I foresee that with this
book, which according to human judgment will be my last
large publication, I will again stand in a certain lone-
liness in theological and Church circles such as I entered
nearly fifty years ago, and that with it I am about to
make a poor exit for myself! Be that as it may! The day
will come when eventually in this matter also one will admit that I was right." One would err if one mistook such
a statement for arrogance; it is the quiet confidence of a
man who has bowed himself beneath the Scriptures in the face

of a long entrenched tradition which he came to believe is
contrary to the Word. If our Protestant Churches are again
to be reformed, as the Roman Church is presently being renewed, not only this book but Barth's theology as a whole
will need to be taken far more seriously than it has. The
Karl Barth I knew is by no means a spent force. And the
formation of the North American Karl Barth Society is evidence of this. Some scholars have been foolish enough to
talk about a post-Barthian era when frankly I see little
evidence that our generation has yet learned from him
what a sermon is. Perhaps it was necessary for us to go
through a period of existentialism and secularism in order
to discover Barth's message.

Coupled with Barth's humility before God was a humility
before his fellowmen. He knew how to listen to others before he spoke. I can confirm Professor T.F. Torrance's
testimony that a visitor to Dr. Barth's home was plied
with far more questions than he could put to his host. In
his theological writings Barth is constantly putting questions to his contemporaries and to the Church fathers. He
patiently and carefully weighed their arguments. He always maintained an immense respect for other scholars,
even for those with whom he strongly disagreed. I recall
that when I first visited Dr. Barth in 1936 I noted a picture of Friedrich Schleiermacher hanging on a wall -- the
early 19th century theologian who has been described as
"the father of modern liberal Protestantism." "Why not?"
said Barth. "He was a good Christian." Barth never wanted
to found a "Barthian" school of theology, much less a new
church bearing his name. In 1963 he gave me a photograph
of himself signed: "Karl Barth--kein Barthianer." (He was
his own severest critic; hence he could make a drastic
change in his view of christology and the sacraments from
Vol. I to Vol. IV in the Church Dogmatics.) He simply
wanted to be an active participant in the work of that
community of teachers and learners which is the Church--
"the school of Christ." Though a member of the Reformed
Church in Switzerland, he came to be recognized as an
ecumenical theologian of the one, holy, catholic Church.

Was Barth a polemical or irenic theologian? If by
polemics is meant plain-speaking, then Barth was polemical.
He could address sharp rebukes to his closest followers.
But he rarely spoke in anger or indulged in invectives.
In all his writings I can think of only five instances.
The most notorious, of course, was his No!, an answer to

Emil Brunner's natural theology, with an "Angry Introduction." But let us recall the opening words of Barth's
preface. "I am by nature a gentle being and averse to all
unnecessary disputes. If anyone, faced with the fact that
he is here reading a controversial treatise, should suggest that it would be so much nicer if theologians dwelt
together in unity, he may rest assured that I heartily
agree with him. Let me also impress upon him that, humanly
and personally speaking, I have nothing against Emil
Brunner....I should like nothing better than to walk together with him in concord, but in the Church we are concerned with truth, and today with an urgency such as
probably has not been the case for centuries."

The time was 1934 when the persecuted Confessing Church
was fighting for its life against the errors of the
natural theology of the "German Christians" -- errors, by
the way, which in other forms were and still are widespread
throughout Christendom!

Barth's humility before God and man was the fruit of a
knowledge not only of his own creatureliness but of his
utter sinfulness. Once again we need to be careful. The
awareness of his sin and guilt was not the result of a
computation of his open and secret misdemeanors (of which,
of course, he was not free) but of his knowledge of the
revelation of the goodness of God in Jesus Christ. In the
light of that revelation he knew that his best works,
above all his piety, are as "a filthy rag." Wherefore, he
could paradoxically affirm that sinful man, inasmuch as he
remains God's creature, is altogether good, and that his
sin is a denial of the goodness of his humanity. His love
of the music of Mozart stemmed from his belief that Mozart,
more than any Church father, had sounded the praises of the
goodness of the Creator and his creation. I recall an un-
forgettable evening in 1958 when the two of us listened to
all four of Mozart's Horn Concerti in his study after we
had discussed theology for three hours! While most of his
contemporaries--existentialists, novelists, artists, and
composers--were giving expression to man's understanding of
the emptiness, meaninglessness and hopelessness of existence, Barth was echoing the praise of the Book of Revelation: "Worthy art Thou, our Lord and God, to receive glory
and honor and power, for Thou didst create all things, and
by Thy will they existed and were created."

Accordingly Barth's dominant characteristics were his
cheerfulness and humor. In the Festschrift for his 70th

146

birthday Heinrich Vogel contributed an article--not without a twinge of reproach--about "Der lachende Barth."
Yes, Barth could laugh, and best of all at himself.
Robert McAfee Brown has given us this delightful quotation. "The angels laugh at old Karl. They laugh at
him because he tries to grasp the truth about God in a
book of Dogmatics. They laugh at the fact that volume
follows volume and each is thicker than the previous one.
As they laugh, they say to one another, "Look! here he
comes now with his little pushcart full of volumes of
the Dogmatics! And they laugh about the men who write
so much about Karl Barth instead of writing about the
things he is trying to write about. Truly, the angels
laugh."[2]
    Barth's uncompromising opposition to natural theology,
that is, to a theology based on a supposed revelation of
God in nature, is well-known. But he could joke about
that too. I remember a walk we had along the seashore at
Aberdeen, Scotland, in 1936. I was plying him with questions about the first article of the Barmen Declaration
and about the Gifford Lectures he was delivering on John
Knox's Confession of Faith. For a moment he didn't hear
me. He was lost in wonder, gazing out to sea. Then he
said: "What did you say? There is the natural theology!"
    His humour and perhaps also his theology is pointed up
by another of his characteristics: his child-likeness.
He would go down to the water's edge, moving forward and
backward, to see if he would get his feet wet as the
waves rolled in. Many years later a group of us were
having breakfast with Dr. Barth at the Holiday Inn in
Dubuque. In the adjoining booth was a young couple with
a child of three or four years. Mimicking the sounds of
a cow, a duck, a cat and a dog, he had the child in gales
of laughter. He was as entranced with her as she was
with him.
    Barth's child-likeness and cheerfulness were expressions,
I believe, of his simple trust in him who said: "Be of
good cheer....I have overcome the world." Consequently
he wrote that theology is "a peculiarly beautiful science.
Indeed, we can confidently say that it is the most beautiful of all the sciences....The theologian who has no joy
in his work is not a theologian at all. Sulky faces,
morose thoughts and boring ways of speaking are intolerable in this science."[3] Theology was for him a joyful
task because its object is the indescribably good news

of "the beauty of the Lord our God" in the humiliation
and exaltation of Jesus Christ. And--in the words of
the poet, John Keats--"a thing of beauty is a joy forever;
its loveliness increases!"

NOTES

1 Ad Limina Apostolorum - An Appraisal of Vatican II.
   John Knox Press, Richmond 1968, p. 9.
2 Portrait of Karl Barth, George Casalis. Transl. with
   an Introduction by Robert McAfee Brown, New York 1963.
   p. 3.
3 Church Dogmatics II/1, p. 656.

THE CONTRIBUTORS

MARKUS BARTH, professor of New Testament and Ancient
Church History at the University of Basel, formerly professor at Pittsburgh Theological Seminary.

ARTHUR C. COCHRANE, professor of Systematic Theology at
Pittsburgh Theological Seminary.

EMILIEN LAMIRANDE, professeur d'histoire du Christianisme
and chairman of the Department of Religious Studies at
Université d'Ottawa.

PAUL L. LEHMANN, professor of Systematic Theology at
Union Theological Seminary in Richmond, Virginia, formerly Charles A. Briggs professor of Systematic Theology
at Union Theological Seminary, New York.

JOSEPH C. McLELLAND, professor of Philosophy of Religion
at McGill University.

PAUL S. MINEAR, recently retired from his position of
Winkley Professor of Biblical Theology at Yale University.

H. MARTIN RUMSCHEIDT, assistant professor of Historical
Theology at the University of Windsor.

MICHAEL WYSCHOGROD, professor of Philosophy at Baruch
College of the City University of New York.

SUPPLEMENTS

FOOTNOTES TO A THEOLOGY

The Karl Barth Colloquium of 1972

edited and with an Introduction by

MARTIN RUMSCHEIDT

Copies may be obtained by sending your cheque for $3.50 to:

SR/CSR Office
Wilfrid Laurier University
Waterloo, Ontario, Canada
N2L 3C5

Name _____

Address _____

_____

City _____ State _____ Zip _____

(A charge of $ .50 will be made if payment does not accompany your order).